SWEET SILVER

SWEET SILVER

Investing For The Ordinary Joe

JOSEPH CHRISTOPHER

To order additional copies of this book, contact:
Xlibris Corporation
1-888-795-4274
www.Xlibris.com
Orders@Xlibris.com
39795

CONTENTS

PREFACE

When I first began thinking of writing a book many years ago on what is a true passion for me—investing and stock trading I dismissed the idea. I thought "there are far more qualified people with high levels of education and broker licenses". "What could I possibly have to say that hasn't already been said". As the years have gone by and I have gained more knowledge it occurred to me that average people, like myself, are longing for advice and input that is down to earth and easy to understand. I realized that I didn't have to have a Ph.D. and talk in big words that can only be understood by a few to write a book that others would find very useful.

Through the years I have invested in many different things, bonds, stocks, coins, CD's, collectables, options, futures, grains, heating oil but it has only been in the last seven years or so I have concentrated on metals. There are several reasons for this which will be detailed in the following chapters. It has been only about three years now that I have turned my focus to silver. The reasons are numerous, but as I have studied and invested in this market, I feel I have something to share with anyone who is willing to listen.

I believe the silver market is so small and misunderstood that it would take less than 1% of the US population to take notice of this market and invest a minimal portion of their investment capital into silver for the price to simply explode. Whether you're a single mom struggling to support your family or a top level executive who is looking for a good place to invest, I feel silver is the best leverage for the money as well as the most secure place to put your savings. I have some very grave concerns about the US economy and the world economy going forward. The US dollar has been steadily declining and should be questioned as a store of value.

Investing is a topic that many find intimidating and even frightening.

It is my hope that putting my experiences to ink and paper will help others gain financial freedom. I am not considered an expert, but one who has been there and done that. This book was written to help not just those with higher education, but also as the title says "ordinary Joe's".

CHAPTER 1

First be Debt Free

The first rule of smart investing is to be debt free. You say "How can I do it?" Well number one is DO NOT LIVE BEYOND YOUR MEANS. If you are making $35,000 a year and driving a Cadillac Escalade and living in a $300,000 house with interest only payments. YOU ARE LIVING BEYOND YOUR MEANS.

We as Americans demand instant gratification; if someone else has it I should be able to have it too! I'm sorry, but this is a recipe for disaster or at the very least bankruptcy. Being debt free first starts by forgetting about what others think and not judging your own self worth by how many nice things you have. This is hard. No doubt about it. And it may mean a loss of friendships. Ask yourself, are they really friends if they are leading you into financial ruin? Where will they be when you lose your house? Hard questions you really need to think about.

Getting by with less will bring you such peace of mind that you can't even imagine. Just think about how much less stress you would have if you had: no car payments, no house payment, a fulltime homemaker, worked less overtime and had money left over each month after all the bills are paid.

I am a Paramedic by trade and work both in the Emergency Room and on a Fire Department transport unit. If I had a silver dime for every time I have seen a patient, often a male, having a heart attack or physiological break down due to stress, I would be retired by now. It has been said that 90% of all ailments that plague us are related to stress. We bring this stress on ourselves by taking on more than we should. Please listen to this advice, take a step back and look at your life. Where can you cut back? You do not want to end up like so many patients I have seen—lots of toys but dead at 45.

It's never too late to start. You can drive a used vehicle. You can limit your kids to just one sport. And you can live in a house that takes less of your paycheck. Please start somewhere, your life does depend on it. To be debt free is the first step in investing; to have excess cash to buy with is the only way to do it. Please DO NOT go into debt to start investing.

Let's take a look at what the Bible has to say about being debt free. First it should go without saying that God would want us to pay our bills. Here is what the scriptures have to say about surety, more commonly known as debt.

Romans 13:8 *Avoid getting into debt, except the debt of mutual love. If you love your fellow men you have carried out your obligations.*
Proverbs 22:7 *The rich man lords it over the poor, the borrower is the lenders slave.*
1 Corinthians 7:23 *You have all been bought and paid for, do not be slave to other men.*
Proverbs 22:26 *Do not be one of those who go guarantor, who go surety for debts.*

Scripture voices strongly that we are to avoid debt. When we go into debt we are presupposing on God's providence or blessing, to purchase something we can't afford, and then expect God to continue giving us enough money for the next 30 years to pay it off. Are you promising away future income that does not belong to you?

When we assume God has blessed us with a new home or car, and we went into debt for it; perhaps it was not his blessing at all. Rather it was our greed combined with the availability of borrowed money in a wicked financial system, meant to enslave us. Maybe we are just pawns tempted into buying something God intends us to wait and save-up for. Where is our patience? Where is our "waiting on God" that is so often preached about? Where is our trust in his provision? Perhaps he wants us to live in a "shack" for a while, or drive an old beater automobile. Where, oh where is our contentment? You need to ask yourself is this good stewardship.

Deuteronomy 28:15 *But if you do not obey the voice of Yahweh your God nor keep and observe all those commandments and statutes of his that I enjoin on you today, then all the curses that follow shall come up with you and overtake you.*

It is my belief that this is what is happening in the world today. The curse is people are becoming "me" centered. The impact on another does not matter. We have strayed badly from Gods laws and we are paying the price.

Deuteronomy 28:43-48 *The foreigner living among you will rise higher and higher at your expense and you yourselves sink lower and lower. He will make you his chattel, you will not make him yours; you will not be the head you will be the tail.*

We used to be the richest country on earth. We lent to other countries. Now we are the great debtor nation. We owe everybody. This disease has infected the people who now think nothing of owing more than they could make in a lifetime.

Do you realize that deficiency laws are still on the books?[1] What this means is if you are unable to pay back what you owe, the bank has the right to sell it. If they do not get what you owe on it, you are responsible for the difference. For example, you loose your job. You say "Oh well I'll just let the bank take it back" (house or car or whatever you have gone into debt for). In good times this may not be a problem. In bad times banks are stuck with many houses. Houses will be sold for whatever they can get for them. So lets say you have a 250,000.00 dollar mortgage, but this mortgage is upside down, in other words the house is no longer worth that so the bank sells it at auction for 100,000.00 leaving a balance of 150,000.00. They would then issue a deficiency judgment against you. So you would no longer have a place to live in and would still have a debt to pay. Think this can't happen, it happened a lot during the great depression and it can and will happen again. If you have a mortgage do you remember all that paperwork you had to sign, that clause is in there trust me. The banks know how to protect themselves, and you would have to pay.

During the depression an uncle of ours owed 9000 dollars on his house. He could no longer make the payments due to a job loss, so the bank started foreclosure proceedings. Being an avid saver he had more than enough in the bank to pay off the house. The problem was that the banks were closed. He could not get his money out. The same bank that held the mortgage would not allow him to take his money out or transfer his money to pay off the loan. Amazing! Instead they took his house. Just simply incredible, and hard to believe, but it did happen. This is one of the many reasons people lost confidence in the banks. It was around this time that the FICA was created and in an effort to help regain public confidence in the US banking system the government would insure your deposits up to 100,000.00 dollars. This was a lot of money back then, but not so today with most houses costing over 200,000.00 dollars. The government has not increased its amount and most Americans don't have 100,000.00 dollars in the bank anyway so I guess it doesn't matter.

Now I would like to take a look at what some famous people have had to say about debt through the years.

The Modern theory of perpetuation of debt has drenched the earth in blood and crushed its inhabitants under burdens ever accumulating.—Thomas Jefferson[2]

If the American people ever allow private banks to control the issue of their currency, first by inflation, then by deflation, the banks ... will deprive the people of all property until their children wake-up homeless on the continent their fathers conquered .... The issuing power should be taken from the banks and restored to the people, to whom it properly belongs.—Thomas Jefferson[3]

History records that the money changers have used every form of abuse, intrigue, deceit, and violent means possible to maintain their control over governments by controlling money and its issuance.—James Madison[4]

Most are not aware that things in this country changed forever in 1913 on a small island off the coast of Georgia called Jekyll Island. In a nutshell, a small group of bankers formed the Federal Reserve Bank and allowed the elitists to rule the day. Their plans have been proceeding ever since and soon

after we went off the Gold Standard and eventually the Silver Standard as well. This is a most fascinating topic but is beyond the scope of this book. To learn more, a "must read" would be the book "The Creature from Jeckyll Island". This book goes into great detail on how all money changed and how the banking cartel took control. The President at the time was Woodrow Wilson who despite many warnings signed the 1913 Federal Reserve Act. A few years later Woodrow

Wilson wrote: "*I am a most unhappy man. I have unwittingly ruined my country. A great industrial nation is controlled by its system of credit. Our system of credit is concentrated. The growth of the nation, therefore, and all our activities are in the hands of a few men. We have come to be one of the worst ruled, one of the most completely controlled and dominated Governments in the civilized world no longer a Government by free opinion, no longer a Government by conviction and the vote of the majority, but a Government by the opinion and duress of a small group of dominant men.*"[5]

If congress has the right under the Constitution to issue paper money, it was given them to use themselves, not to be delegated to individuals or corporations.—Andrew Jackson.[6]

The key to financial success is to not be involved in usury, debt is usury. In days gone by there were places known as debtors prisons. I believe we will have these again. It could be said that those deep in debt are already in their own prison. The wealthy elite of the world, the billionaires are not in debt. They are the ones that loan us into debt. If you have any thought of being wealthy or at least financially well off, you need to start thinking like the elitists. It is easy to sit back and direct our anger at the rich and blame all the maladies of society on them because they have grown rich off the blood and sweat of others, but the fact is they may be following the bible more closely than we are by simply not using debt.

So you say fine and good, but I am so far in debt that I just see no way out. You may be considering a second mortgage. I'm sorry, but this is not an answer to all your troubles and should be a last resort, not the first. Many have gone this route only to find themselves in worse shape in a very short period of time. They pay off all the credit cards, car loans and student loans only to run them all back up again. The solution is not more debt and taking out all the value you have accumulated in your home. The cure is to live within your means today so you can be financially free and stress free in the future. Those of us that live in western culture are addicted to credit and instant gratification. It is fun to be able to buy pretty much anything we want now and pay for it latter. But as many will tell you who have had their homes foreclosed on and found themselves homeless—the piper may come to call some day.

So what can I do? I would suggest starting small. Make a list. Put all your assets (everything you own) on one side. You may be very surprised to find how little you really own outright; something that is 100% paid for. And on the other side all your liabilities or debts. By each liability put the loan interest rate. Credit cards are usually the highest. This is were it gets fun, and it can be fun. Look at your list, home mortgage and student loans are usually the lowest. Here's what I want you to do. Pick the highest interest rate item. That's the one you are going to pay off first. I want you to make the minimum payment allowed on all other loans and with whatever you have left pay on that high interest loan. You should be able to pay this off in a short period of time which will help to give you a feeling of hope, while giving some of that feeling of instant gratification that so many of us have become accustomed too. Now you're set to tackle the next item on your list. It may be a department store credit card at say 22% interest. Now that you have one under your belt you should have a little more capital to pay off this one with. You get the idea. But you need to be determined, and that means closing these accounts when they are paid off. Just think what an awesome feeling it would be to have your home as your only debt and to have all this extra cash to pay down your mortgage. To me this is gratification the other is smoke and mirrors. Make a game out of it with your family. Let the kids know what you are doing and why. We give far too little credit to the ideas that kids can come up with, they are resourceful. Just the other day my four year old came up to me and said "here daddy, here is some money I found so you don't have to work so much".

We all need to strive to be debt free. Get creative, start somewhere. Work to eliminate debt by not living beyond your means. I believe the future for the upcoming generations is very dim if we don't start acting more responsible in this highly critical area.

CHAPTER 2

Get your House in Order

Get your house in order. What I mean by this, of course, is to have your financial house in order. We talked a bit about this in the previous chapter. But I believe there is a lot more to it than just your finances. It's about being able to provide for your family for a period of time if you lost your job. I'm talking about being self reliant. This is one thing you should not bury your head in the sand about. It happens every day. I have seen an ever increasing number of highly depressed and suicidal people in the ER. It is not a joke. Don't be foolish and say it can't happen to me.

Think about this scenario. A 55 year old accountant making $200,000.00 a year loses his job. All his bills are based on making this sum. Big question, where does someone of this age go and find another high paying job like this? Especially when so many other companies are cutting jobs and outsourcing the work for a fraction of the cost. Answer he most likely won't and will either be unemployed or forced to take a much lower paying job.

It scares me to think of how few skills many Americans have beyond their field or occupation. So many I know sit behind a desk in front of a computer and that's all they know. If they had to fend for themselves in say finding a food source for their family when the pizza joint is closed they would be lost.

I bring all of this up to try and get you thinking and preparing a backup plan. If this happened tomorrow how long would you make it? How much cash do you have on hand? How much food do you have available. Do you have any medical supplies on hand? You say I'll have unemployment to run on and besides the government will take care of me. I can just file for bankruptcy. It will be alright. Or this one I've heard a lot. God will take care of me. I do believe he can and will, but we are called to take an active role in our lives.

Bad things do happen. It is one of my hopes in writing this book to get you thinking on a different plane.

I have found it hard to believe how many college graduates have difficulty finding work after they graduate. I remember a few years back, when I took my paramedic class, that there were a number of students with degree's who had to go back and take this class to find a job. Along the same line, I recently saw a posting at work that went something like this-

Open Position
Executive Accounting Supervisor
Minimum Requirements
Bachelor's degree in accounting
Two years experience
CPA preferred
Starting pay $16.35 a hour

It just amazes me, that much schooling and such a relatively meager wage! My point here is that a lot of schooling does not guarantee you a great paying job or steady employment. In a declining economy you need to take a serious look at what is in demand and will be in demand for years to come. Health care I believe fits this bill as well as many government jobs like police, fire and I'm sure many others. Do not become complacent and think your job will always be there. It is very shortsighted if you run up a bunch of debt to buy all the toys and say to yourself "I can make the payments no problem".

You need to take a serious look around you and realize things are not well in our post industrial society. The basket of fudged numbers that our government continues to spew out such as the CPI and the unemployment numbers is just amazing. To be counted as unemployed you have to be collecting unemployment benefits. Once they run out you are no longer counted.[7] It also does not count the large number of people who are under employed by either having to take a job that pays a lot less, or having their hours cut.[8] You need to really use your common sense here and start thinking for yourself instead of what you are being told to think. Now is the time to start preparing your backup plan.

The main topic of this book is silver and why I think it's just the beginning of a great bull market. But I feel I would be remiss if I did not express my thoughts on being prepared for some bad times that might lie ahead. To me one of the worst possibilities a man could be faced with would be the inability to feed, house and cloth his family. This is a prospect I have taken measures to avoid. Getting your financial house in order is just one aspect. Getting your nutritional house in order is also important.

Food should be a high priority. It is so cheap right now, that for a small sum you could easily put away a 6 month supply of can goods, pasta and other non perishables. It may sound radical, but if the dollar continues to loose value food will become harder to obtain in quanties. Whole wheat and rice are great food stores and will last for years. High impact grinders grind 8 cups of kernel wheat into flour in about a minute. This is just one example of becoming a little more self reliant. Another is good old fashion gardening and canning. There are many good web sites that can help you on this road. One that I like is lds.org under provident living they have a food calculator to help decide how much to store and how to store it.

Why are so many people catching on to organic food? Here's what I know. Much of the soil in our country has been over farmed. It has not been rested as stated in the biblical 7 year land rest. It is missing a lot of the nutrients that it once had, such as selenium.[9] So in an effort to get high yields out of their fields many farmers have gone to GMO seed. GMO stands for genetically modified organism which becomes a genetically modified seed. Scientists have engineered seed that is insect resistant and chemical resistant so that they can spray weed killer that will kill everything except that crop. Studies have shown that in the process much of the nutritional value has been lost.[10] [11] Such is the case of the Monarch butterfly which has had its population greatly reduced by this GMO planting. The Monarch feeds on milkweed which commonly grows on the sides of cornfields. Hybrid corn, known as Bt-corn, pollinates like other plants by being wind blown. This yellow sticky pollination spreads to the surrounding milkweed which is then consumed by the butterfly. It has a similar insecticide effect on Monarchs as it has on the corn borer it was engineered to eliminate. The other concern many have is the potential loss in nutritional value of the plant when consumed.[12] Organic farmers are well aware of these facts and I am sure a lot more. Many good web sites exist that discuss GMO seed; some are listed in the back of this book.

Many people take vitamins to boost their nutritional intake. There is a world of difference between brands. First of all, I shy away from any vitamin produced by a pharmaceutical company. Companies that make chemicals, in my opinion, can not be counted on to produce something all natural. Just because it says "all natural" does not mean it is.[13] This is putting a lot of faith in the FDA and the government that they have our health at the top of their list, or is it some lobby group. Here's what you want to look for. What are the vitamins derived from? Are they from plants or are they chemicals. If they are from plants how are they processed? Vitamin C is one example. Many people take it to help with and prevent colds. The label on the bottle of vitamin C says "all natural". But let's take a deeper look. The first ingredient and main ingredient is Ascorbic acid. This is not true Vitamin C. The vitamin C molecule is made up of 4 main substances. Ascorbic Acid is nothing more than the outer coating or shell of the molecule.[14]

Here's one more that I find just amazing. Fluoride is said to prevent cavities. The research is very weak. I saw one study that said it hardened the teeth of a group of school age kids. I am aware of no other studies. So let's follow the money trail. Fluoride is aluminum by-product that is a hazardous waste material and comes out in the production of aluminum. For years metal producers had to pay to have it disposed of. Now they make money off it. Just try to buy toothpaste without fluoride in it or city drinking water without it. This is one chemical that even the best water filters can not take out. You say so what, it can't be that bad for me. Well let's see, first of all it is an aluminum by-product. Studies have shown that aluminum levels in the body have a strong link to Alzheimer's disease as well as others.[15][16][17] In the back of the book are a few web sites to help you do some research on this.

Here is a thought that I want to end this chapter with. If you took 3000 dollars and put it into food for storage would you be further ahead than leaving it in the bank. Let's see. 3000 dollars at say 3% interest in the bank would earn you 90 dollars in interest in a year. If you're like me, you go to the grocery store a lot. You know prices are going up. It is a no brainer that you would be further ahead with food in your pantry. You know you are going to use it. And now you have more peace of mind knowing if the #&*# hits the fan and you lose your job you can feed your family. Remember the Boy Scout rule—be prepared. You need to be a forward thinker and get your house in order for the goldilocks economy we have enjoyed for many years may be coming to an end.

CHAPTER 3

The Bible on Silver and Gold

I'd like to start out this chapter by saying I' am a strong Christian believer who feels all this time spent on earth is a time for growing in holiness and union with the Creator. Having said that this chapter is geared toward showing how God, whether the God of Jewish, Christian, Muslim or any other faith that believes in a supreme being, intended Gold and Silver to be used as money, and for honest weights and measures to be used (Lev 27:16, 2 Kings 7:1, Lev 19:35). It is a abomination to God when dishonest weights and measures are used (Deut 25:15, Prov. 20:10).

For Christians one of the best examples of this is Jesus and the money changers. Christ became very upset when he saw what was going on inside the temple walls, the scales they used were not honest and scripture says He overturned their tables. In Mark chapter11 verse 18 Jesus says "You have turned the temple into a *robbers den.*" It is worth noting that this is the only time recorded in the bible that Jesus became angry.

We are called by God to be honest in our business dealings, paper money is not honest. It can be printed with wild abandon. The reason gold and silver are honest money is because they are rare enough to be considered as valuable this is why lead is not a precious metal, it is plentiful.

There are numerous times gold and silver are mentioned in the bible. It was considered a store of wealth and is often mentioned in the context of kings and their wealth. It is what the Ark of the Covenant was made of as well as the vessels of the sanctuary. Jesus was sold for 30 pieces of silver. The list could go on and on. It is a rare occasion for me to pick up my bible and not find some reference to gold or silver. It was a measure of wealth and enabled people to purchase goods and services. It was the medium of exchange. It was ordained by God, and it is mentioned early on in Genesis Chapter 2 verse 12. (*The gold of this land is pure; bdellium and onyx stone are found there.*)

The standard money used back then was the Shekel or Talent. The Shekel is mentioned numerous times in Leviticus as to the value of things and the Talent is most notably mentioned by Jesus in the parable of the talents. Both measures of wealth were made of silver.[18]

The biblical story of the silver talents becomes more real when you realize that one talent of silver was approximately 75 pounds of silver[19] or 1200 ounces of silver which at today's prices would be 13,000.00 dollars per talent that was a lot of money each servant was entrusted with. If you know the story then you'll remember that one servant was given one talent the second servant was given five talents and the third was given ten talents. So the guy with the 5 talents had 375 pounds of silver or 6000 ounces = $78,000.00 and the last servant who was given 10 talents had 750 pounds of silver or 12,000 ounces = $156,000.00. This master really entrusted these servants with a good deal of his wealth. This truly was a store of wealth.

It is interesting to note as I sit here writing this chapter and thumbing through my bible I stumbled across Proverbs chapter 25, attributed to Solomon who is said to be the richest man who ever lived. It speaks of removing the dross from silver to purify it and compares that to removing the wicked from the kings sight. It is strange to stumble upon this while looking for another passage and it helps to make my point that scripture is full of references to what money should be.

So let's take a look at what scripture has to say about honest weights and measures. Get in your mind the picture of a scale, the type that would have been used in ancient times to weigh gold and silver. The scale would sit on a table and have two plates suspended by chains between a stand. Now picture some gold coins on one side and the same equivalent value in paper money. I think you know what I'm getting at obviously the weight of the gold will make the scale go down. Now take yourself back to the time of Jesus and the moneychangers. What would these Jews have thought if you came with your paper money and placed it on the scales? What kind of look would you get? I think they would have thrown you out of the temple. Now let's think about what Jesus would think. What would He say? You say, well, things were different then, those were biblical times. Jesus would understand. Times are different now. If there is one thing I know about my faith it is this, God never changes. God stays the same, it is people who change. God's laws are not to be altered.

Proverbs 20:23 One weight here, another there, this is abhorrent to Yahweh False scales are not good

Leviticus 19:35 Your legal verdicts, your measures—length, weight and capacity—must all be just. Your scales and weights must be just, a just ephah and a just hin. I am Yahweh who brought you out of the land of Egypt.

Deuteronomy 25:13 You are not to keep two different weights in your bag, one heavy, one light.

Deuteronomy 25:14 You are not to keep two different measures in your house, one large, one small.

Deuteronomy 25:15-16 You must keep one weight full and accurate, so that you may have a long life in the land that Yahweh your God has given you. For anyone who does things of this kind and acts dishonestly is detestable to God.

Here is why I feel paper money is not an honest weight or measure. Whether you are a doctor or a garbage collector you earn a wage. It is paid in paper money. Now let's say inflation is running at 10% which I believe it is or higher despite what they would have you believe, your wage that you earn is worth less and less all the time, in other words it buys less of what you need and this is a form of stealing. If you had been paid in a just weight, such as silver, inflation would cease to exist and when you got a raise it would mean something, not just something to try and keep up with inflation.

I challenge you to pick up a bible and just start thumbing through, there is a lot in there about money and how we are to handle it. As a Christian I am striving to enter heaven one day. None of us really knows exactly what heaven will be like, but honesty will rule the day. We are to be heaven minded and I don't believe theft will be part of daily going ons in heaven.

Additional Scriptures concerning honest weights and measures:

Amos 8:4-6
Mica 6:10-12
Proverbs 11:1
Proverbs 16:11
Proverbs 20:10
Isaiah 1:22

In James chapter 5 verse 3 it says all your gold and silver is rusting away, and the same corrosion will be your own sentence and eat into your body.

The chapter goes on and talks about how this person cheated those who worked for him. First it needs to be said that gold and silver do not rust and the only way they would is if they were mixed with steel. In the same way paper money will decay and is not a long term store of wealth. Only gold and silver were given by God to transfer wealth from generation to generation all else is not an honest weight or measure.

CHAPTER 4

Gold and Silver Real Money

One of my hopes in writing this book is to get people thinking. Not just about making money or becoming wealthy, but to think outside of the norm. To think for yourself and not just think how others want you to think. This chapter is very important in understanding money and were it comes from. Think hard about this next paragraph.

What makes paper money worth anything? Ponder that thought a minute. Stop reading close the book and ponder why a piece of paper can buy things.

OK, so what did you come up with?

Did you say well how about gold and Fort Knox, or how about all the land our government owns or maybe our military might and all the aircraft, tanks, ships, guns, etc. Well that's all nice but the simple fact is that since we went off the gold standard for good in the early seventies our government has printed Trillions, yes that's with a T, of unbacked dollars.[2021] The notes below actually circulated not so many years ago, They were backed by gold and silver, and as they say on them you could go down to your local bank, turn one of these in and receive the face amount in gold or silver coin.

US 5 Dollar Silver Certificate Series 1934

US 100 Dollar Gold Certificate series 1934

You say so what. I can still buy anything I want with paper money. So why should I care if it is backed by anything as long as I can use it. I can't be bothered with the details. You do have a point except for the fact that history has shown what can happen when a currency is allowed to go unchecked. Perhaps the most recent and most compelling example of this is the currency collapse in Argentina in the early 1990's. This crisis has much history to it, but in brief it began with a run on the banks as inflation was running rampant and people wanted to spend their money on tangible items before it lost any more value. The Government of Argentina froze all bank accounts for 12 months and would only allow withdrawals in small amounts. Argentines took to streets in protest and eventually violence broke out and several people died in skirmishes with police this precipitated the fall of the government. An interim government was put in place which implemented a replacement currency. This was pegged to the US Dollar, which is also backed by nothing. The old currency was now worthless and this new currency was quickly losing value. The decline in this currency has recently slowed.[22] From this example you can see it is important to have a currency with some form of tangible backing. No country is immune to a currency collapse.

One other point is that a man who is the head of a household needs to be a forward thinker and plan for the future. He needs to think outside of what he has been taught and indoctrinated with. Just remember the crowd is not always right. You may not be running in the right direction.

What makes money worth anything can be summed up in one word faith. It is only our faith in the US dollar that allows it to be exchanged for goods and services. You may say that is silly, but think about this, if a loaf of bread used to cost 19 cents and now you cant find it for less than 2 dollars, that is inflation. This word is used a lot, but what it really means is the dollar has lost its purchasing power. It simply buys a lot less than it used too. So next time you hear someone talking about inflation just remember what it really means is your paycheck and any money you have in the bank are worth a lot less and buy a lot less than they did a short time ago.

When prices of tangible items like food, cars, houses, gold, silver, copper, gasoline etc . . . Go up they are really not going up. The dollar is going down and will continue to do so as long as the government continues to print paper money with abandon in its effort to keep things afloat.

Think of it this way. Let's say you bought an old house and while cleaning it out in the attic you found 20,000.00 US paper dollars put there during the 1930's depression. This would have been a fortune back then. It could have bought a lot of things say maybe 10 houses, but because it was left in paper it won't even buy a nice car. And let's say you also found a hundred ounces of gold in this attic. Gold was at $35.00 an ounce back then. So it cost this person $3500.00 for this gold. Today it would be worth $70,000.00. That's inflation. Gold has retained its value while paper has not. Here's another thought, if this person had taken his 20,000.00 and put it in gold he could have bought 571 ounces at 35 dollars. Today it would be worth 400,000 dollars. Sounds like that would have been the way to go.

In order to define what money really is we need to define what wealth is.

Most of us would say if you had a million dollars in the bank you would be wealthy or at least well off and this would hold pretty true at the writing of this book. But, my purpose in writing it is to get you to think outside of the way the masses think. It should be very clear from the above example that the almighty dollar has lost a lot of value over the years and shows no sign of slowing down and may even accelerate its losses.

We can all agree that at best, we are going to live about eighty years and then someone else is going to get what we worked so hard for. So I want you to think really hard about what wealth is. I believe it is this. To have all your needs met and to have some fun along the way. I suppose to many it would mean never having to work a regular job again. If you have traveled the world at all, and seen the extreme poverty that exists, you would agree that wealth is having all your needs met. So having said this lets say paper money becomes worthless. What are some of the things you could store your wealth in? Think about your daily needs and what you consume day after day. A sample list is shown below.

Daily Needs
Food
Shelter
Clothing
Transportation
Heat source (firewood, heating oil, propane)
Electricity (alternate source, windmill, generator)
Health care
Protection
Gold, silver

It may sound like a list for survival in a deep woods cabin, but it is not. Think about it, when it comes down to it what makes a man wealthy is his ability to provide for his family under any circumstance. If paper money is not a good store of wealth then what becomes a store of wealth are the things that throughout history have been considered such. We really, really need to learn some lessons from our past.

Notice that gold and silver are at the bottom of the list, yes they are great stores of wealth but "you can't eat gold". It will not mean that much if your standard of living shrinks to a point that you cannot provide the basic necessities of life. After storing basic necessities, you need to get serious about protecting your financial future. Put some of your surplus assets into gold and silver.

Perhaps the most compelling case I have read recently that gold and silver are real money has come from a most unexpected place, that of our past Federal Reserve Chief, Allen Greenspan. In 1966 he wrote *"In the absence of the gold standard, there is no way to protect savings from confiscation through inflation. Gold stands in the way of this insidious process"*. Again in 1999 in testimony before the US House Banking Committee he stated *"gold represents the ultimate form of payment in the world"*.[23]

Here are some additional quotes from others who support the position that "gold and silver are real money" . . .

In 1913 J. P. Morgan stated *"Gold is money and nothing more"*.[24]

Most recently comes some comments from a Canadian banking official

Anthony S. Fell, January 2007.[25]

> *"At the Royal Bank we trade gold bullion off our foreign exchange desks rather than our commodity desks, because that's what it is—global currency"*

> *"It's not prudent for the US to depend on foreign bond buyers to finance domestic consumption"*.

> *"Major currency realignment is coming, and the longer it is delayed, the more the risk of a crisis. You can't hold back the tide."*

> *"To some extent, I regret to say, all paper currencies are becoming somewhat suspect"*.

Gold and silver are real money, but so are many tangible items. Money and wealth in all essence are made up of truly tangible items which are "real money'. Think outside the box you have been in, and realize that paper assets may not be the best place to store your savings. They can and do lose value and they can collapse.

CHAPTER 5

Gold & Silver vs. Paper Money

For most of recorded history silver and gold have been accepted as the premier medium of exchange when you just couldn't barter for something, like the blacksmith shoeing your horse for 2 dozen eggs. If our ancestors came back from the 1800's and found that you could not take a paper dollar to the bank and trade it in on a silver dollar they would spew something out of their mouths like; "Are you stupid? Why have you allowed this to happen? Do you not realize that this paper is worthless and will go the way of all paper monies of the past—into the dung pile?"

It is clearly stated in our constitution Article 1 section 10 [26]; "no state shall make any monies except that of gold and silver coin".[27] This section of the constitution has never been repealed, it is simply overlooked ignored and forgotten about. It could therefore be stated that paper money is not legal tender, but illegal tender according to the US constitution.

Silver makes the most sense as a medium of exchange. It is more plentiful than gold but scarce enough to be a precious metal. Silver was the metal of choice for most day to day transactions in times past and will be again.

It is worth noting that within the US there have been times in our history that the US dollar has become worthless. The first time was in the 1700's. The cost of the revolutionary war was tremdous and the continental government printed paper money in excess of gold to back it. All was well in a short time as we had beaten the brits. The next time was during the civil war. Both sides printed paper money to pay for the war and when it was all over both currencies were worthless.

Again during WWII the war cost us a great deal and the printing presses went into overdrive. The result was a 50% loss of value. A car, home or just about anything else cost nearly double what it had before the start of the war. The dollar has continued to lose value since then as should be obvious to most. Things of tangible value cost a lot more than they did in 1945.[28] It should also be obvious that the money you earn buys less and less every day. Those who save it whether in the bank or under a mattress are losing.

This book is about trading so let's talk about the currency markets and how they come up with the value of the US Dollar. When you look at most charts they compare the Dollar to the Euro or the Yen. It is being compared to other paper monies. What is actually being compared is the annalist's perception of these countries economies. A quick trip to Yahoo Finance will show what the Dollar is worth against most other currencies, but again they are all paper. It is interesting to note that early paper money was clearly redeemable for gold or silver coin, as can be seen on the note below.

US 50 Dollar Gold Certificate series 1934

Another important fact to consider is that paper dollars occur 40,000 times more often than an ounce of gold. So, if all things ever became equal gold would cost 40,000.00 dollars an ounce and silver would not be far behind. Paper dollars are much more common than precious metals. The chart below shows this in great detail.

$$

The Money Chart[29]

$$

1,000,000,000,000:	1 Trillion dollars
1,000,000,000:	1 Billion dollars
1,000,000:	1 Million dollars
$400,000,000,000,000:	Estimated total derivative exposure of all banks in the entire world. (20 x U.S. GDP) (up to $400 Trillion?)
$118,000,000,000,000:	World Global Capital Markets (Stocks, Bonds, &?) Feb 2005 McKinsey Global Inst.
$75,000,000,000,000:	U.S. Govt. unfunded liabilities; social security, etc.
$49,000,000,000,000:	World bond market, Fall 2004 PWL Capital Inc.
$46,000,000,000,000:	Total World Paper Money supply 2004; from M2 & GDP of EU, USA, Japan, & China (see SSR #56)
$45,153,000,000,000:	U.S. Household wealth, as of first quarter, 2004. (Includes Real Estate, and investments) *http://www.pwlcapital.com/website/en/advisors/PWL ToolboxFALL2004.pdf*
$37,000,000,000,000:	Total global equity market capitalization June 2001 UN.ORG
$21,700,000,000,000:	Total global market capitalization of NYSE stocks, Dec '05 http://nyse.com
$21,000,000,000,000:	U.S. bond market, Sept, '03: IAPF treas.gov *http://www.bea.doc.gov/bea/dn/home/gdp.htm*
$12,605,000,000,000:	U.S. GDP, 2005 (3Q) http://www.bea.doc.gov/bea/dn/home/gdp.htm
$10,261,000,000,000:	M3 (money in U.S. banks) Jan '06 http://tinyurl.com/vra0
$8,249,000,000,000:	US debt, 2-23-2006 http://www.publicdebt.treas.gov/opd/opdpenny.htm
$4,000,000,000,000:	Total global market capitalization of Tokyo stocks, Dec '05 http://nyse.com

$3,600,000,000,000: Total global market capitalization of Nasdaq stocks, Dec '05
http://nyse.com

$3,000,000,000,000: Total global market capitalization of London stocks, Dec '05
http://nyse.com

$2,622,000,000,000: Total gold mined in all of history, 150,000 T (4.6 bil oz.) @ $570/oz.
http://tinyurl.com/vrcc

$2,500,000,000,000: Total global market capitalization of Euronext stocks, Dec '05
http://nyse.com

$2,400,000,000,000: U.S. annual budget 2005

$1,200,000,000,000: Total global market capitalization of Deutsche Boerse stocks, Dec '05
http://nyse.com

$754,000,000,000: Total U.S. paper currency & coin in circulation, March 2005
http://www.fms.treas.gov/bulletin/index.html
http://www.publicdebt.treas.gov/opd/opdpenny.htm

$753,000,000,000: Annual U.S. current account deficit (trade deficit) for 2005, (annualized from 1 Q 2005).

$596,000,000,000: U.S. debt increase (true deficit) (Fiscal year '03-'04).
http://www.publicdebt.treas.gov/opd/opdpenny.htm

$400,000,000,000: Total silver mined in all of history: 40 billion oz. @ $10/oz.
http://snipurl.com/93j1

$376,000,000,000: Market Cap of Exxon Mobil (biggest U.S. Corp.) (8-05)
http://finance.yahoo.com/q?s=XOM

$286,000,000,000: Debt of General Motors (biggest U.S. car company) Jan 2006

$149,000,000,000: US gold, 261 mil oz., @ $570/oz.
http://tinyurl.com/vsr9

$110,000,000,000: all the world's gold stocks/equities (Sept. 25, 2005, Denver Gold Conference)

$75,000,000,000: Money flowed into Equity funds in the first quarter, 2004

$26,000,000,000: Market Cap of Newmont July '05 (biggest gold company in the world)

$8,226,000,000: all the world's "primary" silver stocks (80 of them on this list, as of June 25, 2004)—my own data—J. Homell.

$7,000,000,000: annual flow of money "lost" in Las Vegas while gambling.

$4,000,000,000:	Total annual ATM penalty fees—$13/year per household http://redtape.msnbc.com/2005/10/now_even_atm_de.html
$3,500,000,000:	**350 mil oz. of "identifiable" silver bullion left in the entire world, according to GFMS @ $10/oz.**
$1,300,000,000:	130 million oz. of silver needed by the Barclays Silver ETF: feared to cause a silver shortage by the SUA.
$720,000,000:	72 mil oz. of "registered" NYMEX silver bullion (1-05-05) @ $10/oz. http://www.nymex.com/sil_fut_wareho.aspx
$266,000,000:	40 million oz. of silver purchased for investment, in 2004 at $6.66/oz.
$75,000,000:	Limit 7.5 mil oz. of silver @ $10/oz. (limit of 1500 contracts per trader) at NYMEX
$15,000,000:	Limit 1.5 mil oz. of silver @ $10/oz. (potential 1 month delivery limit) at NYMEX
$7,500,000:	Limit .75 mil oz. of silver @ $10/oz. (over 150 contracts and you must reveal who you are) at NYMEX
$100,000:	Limit of FDIC insurance per bank account.
$5,000:	Limit of average cash withdrawl from small town banks, without ordering cash in advance.
$300:	Limit of average ATM daily withdrawl
$10:	Approximate amount of silver available per person in the U.S. at $10/oz., given 300 million oz., if that is available.

$$

How do we find the value of gold and silver? Kitco.com is a good site. It will show the spot price of gold and silver in US Dollars. What does this really mean? Can I go out and buy it for that? The answer is no. There is a premium, about 25 dollars over spot for gold and 1.50 dollars for silver, unless you buy junk silver. And there is the cost of shipping and insurance, unless you have a dealer nearby. My question would be this, "How available is it?" A $3000 dollar order, of silver is not a hard order to fill. I have heard that dealers are having a hard time filling larger orders. Silver is a small and tiny market especially when compared to the bond, stock or currency markets, which are in the trillions of dollars. One must remember that the electronic medium can say what something is worth but the real question is availability. Is it available for what they say? Or, is it available at all? Is anyone willing to sell? And if they are, are they willing to accept paper for real money?

I believe that the US dollar will become worthless someday. I also believe that it will be slow in progression. The US dollar will continue to lose purchasing power and our standard of living will slowly be eroded. I believe some very hard times lie ahead of us. Those of us who become lean and make the sacrifices now will survive. Those who ignore the warning signs will suffer as so many have in history. Be assured that the media will do all that it can to instill public confidence in the dollar. It should be obvious to those conducting commerce, that what you need for your daily bread, so to speak, is costing more and more every day.

So my point is this, those who ignore history are doomed to repeat it. Whenever paper money experiments have been tried throughout history they have failed. Perhaps you are familiar with the story of the German Mark.[30] In the days following Germany's loss in WWI the German government began printing its currency with wild abandon in an effort to rebuild the devastated country. It got so bad that the treasury simply began adding zero's to the notes and thus turned hundred Mark notes into million Mark notes.[31] Out of this comes the now famous story of the man who took a wheel barrel full of this money to the local bakery to buy bread. The baker refused the worthless paper money. When the man came out to retrieve his money he found a pile of cash on the ground and his wheel barrel missing. Tangible useful items will always be worth more than paper with ink on it.

History has shown us that silver and gold were consistently used as a medium of exchange. It was the intention of the founding fathers of our country that gold and silver coin would be used to conduct commerce. Silver is rare and in short supply, especially when compared to the vast amount of paper investments available. Paper money that you work for buys less and less every day. Those who save in it are losing and will not get back what is lost.

CHAPTER 6

Silver vs. Gold

How could anyone think that silver could be better than gold? It's not that silver is better than gold it's that silver has the greatest percentage potential to make you money. Consider this fact, silver occurs 20 times more often in the earths crust than gold (that is of all the elements that the earth is made of) and yet the price ratio of silver to gold is around 50 to one. In other words it takes 50 ounces of silver to buy 1 ounce of gold. Leverage will be your friend as the markets pick up these facts.

There are many reasons why I feel silver is a better investment than gold. The most compelling argument would be that it has always been considered the poor mans gold. As the masses try to move into hard assets and gold shoots higher, silver will still look affordable to the average person even though it may have gone up a lot more on a percentage basis than gold. Take this example in 1980 gold went from 150 dollars an ounce to a high of 850 dollars. Silver went from 2 dollars an ounce to 50 dollars. Gold sounds a lot more exciting, but percentage wise silver went up a lot more. You need to think in terms of percentage. When an item goes from say 2 dollars to 10 it is a much greater increase than when a hundred dollar item goes to two hundred. The later sounds more impressive but in reality the hundred dollar item went up 100% but the 2 dollar item went up 500%. Or it might be simpler to say the hundred dollar item doubled and the two dollar item went up five times.

This is another reason I like silver so much. When it goes up say just 50 cents it is a much greater increase than when gold goes up 20 dollars. I maintain that silver still will give you a better bang for your buck. Gold and silver have historically been the great stores of wealth and they still are by those in the know. It's the masses that do not understand it.

As of the writing of this book the train has not left the station on the silver market. It is like a skyscraper (stocks and bonds) vs. the pigeon that nests on it (silver). The silver market is so small that very little investment interest would cause it to go up. As this fever catches, as I believe it will, this market will go to the moon. Lets take a look at why this is such a tiny market and why it would take very little to make it fly.

Of all the silver currently being mined and brought to the market, 80% of it is a by product of gold, copper, lead and zinc mining.[32] In other words, the lion's share of silver that is consumed is there because of companies whose main focus is not silver. If we look at the combined production of the three major silver mining companies Coeur d'Alene mines, Helca and Pan American their combined silver production for 2003 was 32.6 million ounces. This is only 3.7% of all silver mined for that year. Divide that into 880 million ounces that was consumed in that year and you begin to get the picture. Silver miners themselves are very tiny as compared to demand and overall silver brought to the market. So it could be said that if demand for the primary base metals, copper, zinc and lead were to slow these miners would mine less hence bringing less silver to the market and placing a even tighter squeeze on the silver market.[33]

My favorite silver stock among the majors is SSRI, Silver Standard Resources. It is not at all the major producer, but it is ranked number one in ounces in the ground at 962 million ounces in 15 locations around the world. If SSRI were able to bring all their silver out of the ground in one year (which is impossible) they could only supply the market for 13 months.[34] Then they would be completely out of silver. This is a major reason why the majors are so hot after the junior miners. The major miners do their own exploration, but what better way to keep your business going than to simply buy up small exploration companies that have already made the discoveries. Takes a lot of the risk out of it for the majors, and this is the number one reason I am so bullish on these tiny exploration companies.

You don't have to know very much about investing to realize that nothing gets Wall Street more excited than take over's, or tender offers from major companies for smaller ones. Often the sky is the limit on how high the stock price will go and the percentage gain can be astounding. It is my firm belief that as investors begin to catch the silver fever and demand explodes major mining companies will bid up the prices of these small mining interests in a desperate effort to bring more metal to the market. The key I believe is to be well positioned in these exploration companies and sit tight.

The last point that needs to be made on why silver is such a tiny market is to compare it to the other investments that catch investor's money. First, the world bond market is estimated at 50 trillion. Next the world's paper money supply is estimated at 50 trillion, combined that's 100 trillion in paper money.[35] That's a lot of paper that is backed by nothing but a persons trust in the government that prints it and the faith that it is worth something and is acceptable to others as a medium of exchange for goods and services.

The point I am trying to make is how small this market really is and if just 1% of the world's money tried to move into silver it could not even be done. Do the math. That's one trillion dollars trying to buy silver. There is at best 400 million ounces of silver available for investment. This would not even come close to filling this order. Prices would skyrocket. Everybody and their brother would be cashing in all the silver they could get there hands on; tea sets, silverware, old coins. It all would still not fill this order.

The above example does not include the hundreds of trillions of dollars invested in the world stock markets. As money moved out of these and into mining stocks and silver bullion the combined pressure on the price, but more importantly the availability of silver, will be amazing to watch.

One more big reason I feel it is wise to be very bullish on the future of silver is its many healing properties. Colloidal silver products have been available for many years and ancient people were aware of its healing properties and anti-microbial benefits. Unlike other metals silver has a great future in the medical field. It is currently in wide use as a wound treatment and is the number one treatment of burns in use today.

But this topical use is just the tip of the iceberg. The real story is its oral use as an antibiotic. Wide spread knowledge of this use has largely been kept from the public by the major drug companies who cannot make enough profit on a product that can cure so many illnesses and disease. So at least for the time being its uses will be known to the homeopathic crowd.

The specific product I would like to talk about is known as ASAP by biotech labs tradable through Clifton Mining Corporation. What sets this product above other colloidal silver preparations is the way it is made. ASAP is a silver nano-partical product, it is metallic silver as opposed to other colloidal silver products that use an ionic silver composition. The metallic silver radiates energy in very narrow wavelengths between ultra-violet "A" and ultra-violet

"B". This radiation is harmful to pathogens, which is instrumental in the exceptional antimicrobial efficacy of this product.[36]

Yet one more use for silver that greatly effects our health is its use as a disinfectant, particularly in hospitals. It has been proven to kill things that other disinfectants can't. (Including bleach).[37]

Have you ever heard the term born with a silver spoon in their mouth? What most don't realize is what it was really referring to was that past generations knew that silver had bug killing ability and was used to help prevent illnesses.[38] There are even stories of people sucking on silver dollars when they felt sick. They may not have called it an antibiotic but they knew it made them feel better. The future for silver is especially bright. You might say this is a once in a lifetime opportunity, but I would say it is a once in human history opportunity.

CHAPTER 7

Coins Numismatic vs. Bullion

C oin collecting is a form of investment that should be done either on a very small scale or by those who already have some bullion in their possession. Numismatic coins are coins that have collector value. They only made so many of a certain coin at a certain mint in a certain year. These are just a few of the things that could make a coin valuable. Perhaps the most important is the grade of the coin. Essentially what that means is how much wear does the coin have as it circulated through the years.

If you have never purchased investment grade coins before the first lesson would be to buy only slabed coins. Slabed coins are in a holder with a grade noted on it, of say MS64, from a coin grading service such as PCGS.[39] What this means is that a professional coin grader, usually three of them, have examined this specific coin and have assigned a grade to it, then placed it into a special airtight holder. There is often a very fine line between grades which is usually not visible to the naked eye. A slight scratch can mean the difference of hundreds or even thousands of dollars. Coins are bought and sold every day on EBay[40]. If you have never bought coins before it can be very easy to be taken. Collectors, in the know, demand that a coin be authenticated by a grading service. These encapsulated coins trade more readily than those that are not and in some cases can be as liquid as bullion. Just be sure it has been graded by a well known company. It certainly can be said that a slabed coin has two things going for it. It has collector value as well as the gold or silver metal value. The Morgan Silver Dollar and the Walking Liberty Half Dollar are among the most popular of all collectable coins. Keep in mind that investment grade coins are long term investments.

So, what do I mean by bullion. A bullion coin or bar can come in various increments. Gold American Eagles are arguably the most popular gold bullion coins. Minted by the US Mint they come in increments of 1/10 oz, 1/4 oz,

½ oz, and 1oz.[41] They generally command a premium of 15 to 25 dollars an ounce over the spot price of the day.

Silver Eagles are one way to buy silver. They come in 1oz size only[42], and sell for around $1.25 to $1.50 over spot so in my opinion they are not the best way to acquire silver. Silver bars from Engelhard[43], I think may be better as they sell very close to spot. The best way in my opinion is junk silver. Junk silver is old coins that have circulated a lot and have little or no collector value. Below is a run down on the percentage of silver in US & Canadian coins.

Percent Silver in US coins

Half dollar: 1964 90% silver, 1965-70 40% silver and 1971 on 0% silver.[44]

Quarter: 1964 90% silver, 1965 on 0% silver.[45]

Dime: 1964 90% silver, 1965 on 0% silver.[46]

Percent Silver in Coins		
US Coins		
1964	90% silver	Half dollar, quarter, dime
1965 to1970	40% silver	Half dollar
	0% silver	Quarter, dime
1971	0% silver	Half dollar
Canadian Coins		
Pre- 1964	80% silver	Half dollar, quarter, dime

Canada also eliminated the silver content in their coins in 1964. Pre-1964 Canadian coins had 80% silver. 1971 marked the end to any restraint on the money system as any cheap metal could be used. Sorry if you were under the delusion that we still had silver in our coins.

Most dealers sell silver at a multiple x face value. That is a quarter with a face value of 25 cents is worth a multiple because it has silver in it, so say it may be worth 10 times face value or $2.50 due strictly to its value for silver content. The following chart contains the breakdown in silver content for pre-1965 US Coins.

Coin	Pure Silver (oz.)	Qty required to make 1 oz.
Dime	.07234	14 dimes
Quarter	.18084	6 quarters
Half dollar	.36169	3 Half dollars
Silver clad (40% silver) Silver halves (1965-70)	.1479	7 Silver clad halves
Silver dollar*	.77344	1 ½ Silver dollar (rough est.)

47

* These however are not sold as commonly as junk silver as they have more collector value. The last one minted was the 1935 Peace Dollar.

That's the breakdown in a nutshell with one exception during WW II the US was in desperate need of nickel so the Nickel was made out of silver and copper from 1942 through 1945. It contained .560 oz copper .350 silver and .09 manganese.[48]

Platinum is another investment grade metal, but commands a price that is currently double that of gold. It is available in the same increments as gold eagles: 1/10, 1/4 ½ and one ounce.[49] They are beautiful coins but should be considered only by those who have a lot of money to spend and only after one has a substantial cache of silver and gold.

When determining where to store your wealth the best place is in gold and silver bullion for the foreseeable future. If you desire to collect numismatic coins you should already have some bullion in your possession and intend to keep them long term.

Chapter 8

Silver Stocks vs. Silver Bullion

One of the motivators in writing this book was the large sums of money that can and will be made in trading in and out of silver mining stocks. But that having been said, it is my strong belief, that one should have a substantial amount of your portfolio in hard assets. Something which is held in your possession and you can hold in your hands.

In today's marketplace most everything is electronic. Most brokerage accounts are just an electronic entry. Very few people ever take possession of a paper stock certificate. Even if you did it's still just a piece of paper with some ink on it that says you own a small portion of a company that may or may not exist in the future.

How willing are you to put your financial future in these people's hands? If you have your nest egg all wrapped up in an electronic entry there is nothing tangible to call your own.

I am not a wealthy man, far from it, but we can learn a lot from those who are and how they got there. One of the first things we learn is that they are diversified; they do not hold all of their wealth in paper currency or stocks. Think about it. Why do we hear of rare coins being scooped up by these billionaires?[50] Or how about rare paintings, Rembrandt's, Picasso's and such. It is a store of wealth. You and I most likely will never buy a Picasso or an 8 million dollar coin, but how about silver. It is a great store of wealth that almost anyone can afford. A few ounces of silver may be the best thing you could ever do for your family.

You need to start somewhere and it my strong belief that you would be much farther ahead to place some cash into this asset class (silver) rather than dumping more and more money into your 401k. 401k's go down and down in value, not to mention purchasing power.

Some years back a broker I had at the time talked me into buying a basket of stocks his firm was pushing, saying they were sure to go up in value. Well you probably already guessed what happened, you got it, they tanked. I was going through some papers a few weeks back and found one of these I hadn't sold. It was a very sharp looking stock certificate with a sort of Greek Gothic scene on it. The name of the company was Asia Pulp and Paper. So curiosity got the best of me and I looked it up thinking ooh maybe its worth something now, well it was alright. Ready for this—.0005 per share. I had 200 shares, think I paid around 9 dollars a share. Not exactly one of my best investments. It was around this time, when all these stocks went down, that I decided I could do a much better job investing on my own. I started making decisions based on my own research, and not by being talked into a stock that some millionaire was trying to get out of. The vast amount of free information that is available, on the internet has led me to make my own decisions about my family's financial future.

It is my opinion that the only reason to buy a silver or gold mining company stock is the expectation that it will go up faster in dollar value than the underlying metal. Otherwise you would be better off just buying some silver bullion on the open market. It is my strong suggestion that long before you place a dime in a trading account that you have a fair amount of metal in your physical possession. How much is up to you, but I think it should go without saying the more the better.

CHAPTER 9

Where They Hide

When it comes to stocks there are so many little start up companies that it could boggle the mind. The trick is to see through the mud and find the good ones. Like a scuba diver in murky water clear vision is the key. My hope is to give you that 20 /20 vision. In previous chapters we have talked about why I feel silver is the best place to park your reserve-surplus assets. Now I want to talk about how to find good silver companies.

Stocks can be broken into three types; large cap, medium cap, and small cap. This is the market capitalization of the company. In simplistic terms this tells you the size of the company. For ease of understanding I want to refer to mining companies as small, medium, large, or exploration.

A large mining company would most likely be a company that has been around a while with a proven record of bringing a lot of metal to the marketplace and would have mines all over the world. A medium one would also be a large producer but just simply not as big. A small one may only have one property or just a few but is a producer to some extent, with perhaps a few exploration properties. Finally an explorer would be just that, a company still either drilling or in the geological mapping phase, but with no mine and likely in need of financing to build one.

One of the first things I look for in a mining company is whether it hedges. This means that it has sold forward its metal at today's prices. In my opinion a company that hedges is not forward thinking and does not give its shareholders the best chance to make a profit. I do not recommend companies that hedge. However it is often difficult to determine if a company has hedged as this information is not always disclosed to investors.

For starters I feel you are head and shoulders above the rest when you start with silver. Here is why. Let's say the economy crashes or just takes a severe downturn. Where do you want your money to be? Let's say you had 100% of your investments in computer stocks thinking technology was the way to go. Now the economy crashes, what do you think is one of the first things people will cut back on? The average Joe is going to be concerned about feeding his family not buying a new computer or the latest electronic gadget. Now, let's say you played it safe and bought the big blue chip companies GM, IBM, Ford, Dell, Microsoft, 3M, Wal-Mart, and Home Depot. And the same thing happens are you in any better shape? Will People buy and invest in these companies in a market downturn?

Now let's say you bought some small silver mining companies like I am recommending in this book. If the market crashes, there is a very good chance that these will go down in value as investors dump all stocks. But this is how I look at it, would you rather own a stock of a company that produces something that most no longer need or can afford? Or, would you want to own something everybody wants and may be able to afford a little. These little mining companies own a lot of land with metals in the ground. It won't take long for the market to wake up and realize this. The trick is to already be invested in these small companies before any of this happens. The upward movement in these stocks I believe will be spectacular. What I am really talking about here is leverage. When you buy a stock that has a lot of proven reserves still in the ground, this is leverage. Get a lot for a little.

We need to answer the question "where do small silver mining companies hide?" Well first off they hide very well because silver and all mining stocks in general are below the radar of most investors and for sure most annalists. You will not see any of these stocks mentioned in major investment newsletters or online financial services. To the contrary, most investment gurus would probably try to talk you out of investing in metals. So you have to work a little harder to find them. I have found most of mine through metal investment newsletters and online discussion groups both of which are in the chapter on Web sites.

When you do your research think about the following keys:

o   Find small producer's and exploration companies that have a little bit of a track record, maybe have had good drill results on a particular hole and have several more drilling projects going on. Also look at the area they are drilling. Is it an area that has known silver reserves or are there producing mines in the area?

o   Find a company with silver in its name. Seems kind of silly but think about it, if you as a new investor to this market heard all the hype as silver began to take off you might jump on your computer and do a search using silver as a key word. Therefore these might be some of the first companies to take off.

o   Are they in a safe area? Is the country in the midst of a civil war or under a dictatorship or are they located in a stable region like Canada?

o   Is the metal difficult to mine? Is it in Antarctica or some very remote place with no roads?

o   How deep is it in the ground? Is it the best potential of all, an open pit mine?

Again at this point in time this is such an undervalued and unnoticed market that the downside I feel is very low. These stocks are well hidden from most investors as many of them trade on the Canadian exchanges as well as being based in Canada. They are not well known and do not make many headlines, but in retrospect who had ever heard of Microsoft in the 1980's. So, where do they hide? Do some research; spend some time investigating the companies. The key to being a good investor is to find hidden stocks and be in them before the masses get in.

CHAPTER 10

Day Trading vs. Buy and Hold

Most of us who have been around awhile have heard the fantastic stories of people who made millions day trading stocks. This was most prevalent during the dot com era of the 90's when it was easy to buy the new kid on the block stock hold it for a few days and then sell it for a nice profit.

Well I don't think I'm mistaken in saying those days are over. Sure there are still people who make a living day trading stocks, but the numbers are far less than they used to be.

Remember the days when everybody and their brother it seemed were making money trading internet, computer and electronic stocks? It almost seemed foolish not to jump in and buy some. Everybody was doing it. Then came the crash, also known as the tech wreck and all was not well in internet land.[51] What happened? In my opinion this was an example of greed gone wild. The fact was that many of these companies had no infrastructure. In other words they were run out of a basement or rented office space, with a few computers connected to the internet. They stood very little chance of ever showing a profit. Investors ran their share prices up to levels that made them more valuable than some very large corporations who had been in business for many, many years. It took a while, because Wall Street has a poor and short memory, but investors finally woke up and realized that profits do matter and a lot of these little companies made big by euphoria would need 10 years or more to show a profit.[52]

I strongly believe that silver as well as most all metals will be the stock darlings that the dot com's once were, but the big difference will be that these companies do have infrastructure as well as a tangleble product that is in high demand. The dot com's had neither. That is not to say that euphoria for these stocks won't push the share price past what these companies profits will support bringing on a big correction. But, the difference is they have metal in the ground and in storehouses, as opposed to an idea broadcast on the internet.

So having said all that lets talk about some trading strategies. What I would propose as a good strategy would be somewhere in between a day trader and a buy and hold person. This is what I mean and why I think it will work for you. Unless you are someone who is very seasoned at trading stocks and have hours and hours of spare time to sit in front of a computer you should not consider day trading. By the same token if you buy stocks and never sell them, in other words just forget about them this can also be a costly strategy. In 1999 Ford stock was selling at 53 3/8. As of this writing Ford is in the 8 dollar a share range. So let's use a hypothetical example, say a Ford retiree had 100,000.00 in Ford stock when he retired in 1999 that he had acquired through the years. If he was a "buy and hold type" that stock would be worth 15,008.00 today. So clearly this would not have been a good strategy on this stock.

I would propose that the best strategy would be to be a weekly trader. One who watches several stocks, but is only invested in a select few at any given time. That is not to say that you shouldn't buy some stocks and hold them for a long time. What I am saying is to be a good investor you need to be diligent and watch your stocks closely, so you don't end up watching it go from 53 to 8 as in the above example. Sure it may come back, but the question is will it come back in your lifetime? Another thought is the amount of time that it ties up capital that could be used to buy stocks with more upward potential.

Some may call my strategy the rolling stock strategy and in a way that's what it is, but not exactly. Here's how it works, lets say you buy stock A for $1.25 a share, you buy 1000 shares for a cost of 1250.00 + 7 dollar commission = $1257.00. Four days latter the stock is at $1.62. You sell for a nice profit of $356.00 in four days. 1000 shares x $1.62 = $1620 - 7 dollar commission = $1 613.00 - $1257.00 = $356. And it puts $1613.00 back into your account for the next trade. This is just one trade and the stock only went up 37 cents.

So lets say you can afford to invest more than $1200.00 as in the example above and you open a online trading account with $5000.00. You can now diversify a little. Let's say you have been doing a little research on your own, checking out a lot of silver mining and exploration companies and you have narrowed it down to a top 10. As a new investor I would recommend that you never invest in more than 3 or 4 companies at a time unless you have a lot of time to spend watching them, but even then you can lose your focus.

So you pick three companies you think are best for the money and have roughly $1600.00 to invest in each.

- ✓ CFTN it's trading at .65 a share so you can buy 2460 shares for a cost of $1599.00 + 7 dollar commission = $1606.00
- ✓ SDRG it is trading at $1.22 a share so you can buy 1310 shares for a cost of $1598.20 + 7 dollar commission = $1605.20.
- ✓ SVL it is trading at .87 so you can buy 1840 shares for a cost of $1600.80 + 7 dollar commission = 1607.80.

On your first trade CFTN. This shoots up fast in two days it's at .90 and you sell for a nice profit of $601.00. 2460 shares x .90 =$2214 less 7 dollar commission = $2207 back into your account, take away your original investment of $1606.00 leaves your profit of $601.00

Your second trade SDRG takes three weeks to get to a good profit point and you sell at $1.75 for a good profit of $680.30. I think you have the math down by now, but you may want to check me.

Your last trade is SVL, you have been watching it and it just not moving much, goes up 2 cents then down 2 cents so you decide to just hold it.

Here is were I would like to make my point about buying and holding stocks. The first point would be that yes you did buy this stock in the hopes it would go up quickly as the others did and you could walk away with your profit. Keep this in mind I am recommending metal stocks that have tangible value. You own a small piece of this metal company and to me this is far better than owning any other type of stock. Therefore I never feel bad when the stocks I buy don't go up right away and maybe lose some value. You still own the best investment around. The second point would be that if you sold the stock now it could jump up in two days and you would not be in it. This has happened to me more times than I can count, so often, patience is the order of the day.

So let's look at our performance for our first month of trading

- ✓ CFTN Profit $601.00 back in to account $2207.00
- ✓ SDRG Profit $680.30 back into account 2285.50
- ✓ SVL No profit yet, down 2 cents at .85 $1564.00 still in account

Total profit for the month $1281.30 and a balance in your account of $6056.50. Not bad for your first month of trading and you have more to trade with than when you started. Now you can go back to your top 10 list and look for entry points or you could just wait and see if your first two trades come back down to where you bought them the first time or close to it.

In case this seems a bit complicated lets look at how easy it can be. When you use an online broker it is very easy to set your entry points and sell points. Let's say you're looking at MMG and it is currently trading at $2.85, but you think a good entry point would be $2.50. You would simply go to their trading forum place a buy order for a set number of shares at your set price. Place the order as GTC which means good till cancelled it enters the order and stays active until the stock price of $2.50 is hit and the order fills. You now own the stock at your set price and can turn around and immediately set a sell order at say $3.00 and the platform does the rest. This is what I like best about online trading, it takes very little time and you don't have to watch the stocks constantly. Most of your time should be spent doing research on new metal stocks to add to your portfolio or possible buy list.

Let's take this step by step.

The silver stock your interested in has a recent trading range between $1.25 and $1.75. As you look at it you notice it appears to be on its way down but closed today at $1.33. Now let's say you are like a lot of us and work a lot of hours. So you don't get to your computer till 7 or 8 at night. No problem you simply go in and place a GTC order. Here's how it works. You want in at $1.25 and want to buy 2000 shares.

Here's what it would look like:

Buy
2000 shares
SDRG (symbol)
Limit (order type)
$1.25 (limit price)
Good until canceled (duration)

You would now click review order.

It will now bring up a screen that summarizes what you are going to do, the total cost of the trade, and two choices.

| Place Trade | Change Order |

So you're happy with it so you place the trade.

Your page now will show a trade queued for the next business day and will stay in force until it is filled. It takes you three days to get a fill and you notice it filled early in morning trade at your price of $1.25 and closed that day at $1.31. The market is closed again as it is 10pm, but now you want to place your exit trade. Simply click on the symbol SDRG (it will be underlined as a link) Click trade.

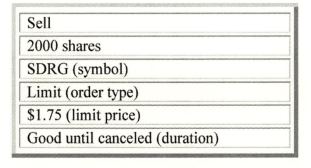

| Sell |
| 2000 shares |
| SDRG (symbol) |
| Limit (order type) |
| $1.75 (limit price) |
| Good until canceled (duration) |

Click

review order

It will bring up a screen that shows what order proceeds would be.

2000 shares SDRG @ $1.75 = $3500.00

Click

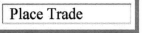

Place Trade

It is now in there and will be until the stock hits your set limit order.

The beauty of this is you don't have to constantly watch your stocks or ever be around during trading hours which are 9:30am till 4: pm Eastern Standard Time (when most of us work).

Your sell order fills 2 weeks later at your set price of $1.75.

Now you could do a couple of things, you could look at your top 10 list and see if there is anything that is trading at the bottom of its recent trading range or you could just place the same trade again on SDRG to buy it at $1.25 again. Who knows it could come back down quickly and even if it doesn't you still have $3500.00 in your account until the order fills and you don't have to watch it.

So let's say you place this trade.

Buy
2800 shares (you are now able to buy 2800 shares with $3500.00)
SDRG (symbol)
Limit (order type)
$1.25 (limit price)
Good until canceled (duration)

Your buy order fills in a week and a half at the set price of $1.25

You go right back in and place your sell order as above @ $1.75.

It fills 3 weeks later at $1.75 for a profit of $1400.00 and puts $4900.00 back into your account.

Here's how it could look if you kept doing it.

$4900.00 buys 3920 shares @ $1.25 sold @ 1.75= $6860.00
$6800.00 buys 5488 shares @ $1.25 Sold @ $1.75= $9604.00
$9604.00 buys 7683 shares @ $1.25 Sold @ $1.75= $13,445.60
$13,445.00 buys 10756 shares @ $1.25 Sold @ $1.75 = $18,823.00
$18,823.00 buys 15059 shares @ $1.25 Sold @ $1.75 = $26,353.00
$26,353.00 buys 21082 shares @ $1.25 Sold @ $1.75 = $36,894.00
$36,894.00 buys 29515 shares @ $1.25 Sold @ $1.75 = $51,652.00
$51,652.00 buys 41322 shares @ $1.25 Sold @ $1.75 = $72,313.00
$72,313.00 buys 57850 shares @$1.25 Sold @ $1.75 = $101,238.00
$101,238.00 buys 80991 shares @$1.25 Sold @ $1.75 =$141,734.00
$141,734.00 buys 113387 shares @$1.25 Sold @ $1.75 =$198,428.00
$198,428.00 buys 158742 shares @$1.25 Sold @ $1.75 =$277,799.00
$277,799.00 buys 222239 shares @$1.25 Sold @ $1.75 = $388,919.00
$388,919.00 buys 311135 shares @$1.25 Sold @ $1.75 =$544,487.00
$544,487.00 buys 435589 shares @$1.25 Sold @ $1.75 =$762,281.00
$762,281.00 buys 609824 shares @$1.25 Sold @ $1.75= $1,067,193

That's One Million sixty seven thousand one hundred and ninety three dollars. It took 18 sell trades to make this happen. If this stock rotated once a month like this in 18 months you would have made over one million dollars with very little effort.

Another point would be that not only can you place trades after hours but on the weekend as well. So say instead of watching the football game on Saturday or Sunday you do your research, place your trades at a limit price and they go into action while you're at work on Monday.

One reason I really like using pre set sell orders is that if a company should have some fantastic results that it announces after the close of trading that stock will undoubtedly run up in morning trading. But the real potential is if it opens much higher than you had your sell order in at it will sell at that price. Brokers commonly refer to this as sell at set price or better. So let's say on the above example you had your sell order at $1.75. At the close of the market SDRG announces it is a takeover target and the stock opens at a higher price, let's say $2.75. The stock will sell at that higher price. So it gives you the opportunity to capture a overnight run up on the morning open before everyone else jumps in and sells. It also allows you to lock in profits before the stock dips back down again. You now could buy back in again. So all this could take place without you having to even look at your account.

As you place trades it is very important to keep a written record of them. This will help you to see how you are doing and keep you motivated in your trading. It should be fun! Like following your favorite sports team, keeping track of each stock as you trade in and out of them can be both rewarding and exciting. On the following page is an example graph that I use for keeping track of my trades.

Investment Log										
Ticker	Company	Buy Date	Price	Quantity	Total Out	Sell Date	Price	Total In	Gain/Loss	%
SDRG	Sil. Dragon	10/26/2006	$1.25	2000	$2,507.00	11/12/2006	$1.75	$3,493.00	$986.00	39%

You must keep in mind that as the price of silver goes up these stocks will experience what is known as higher highs and higher lows. What this means to you, is if you see a stock you have been trading like this never coming back down to $1.25 and going way past $1.75 but still doing decent rolls you need to figure out new entry and exit points. What I'm trying to show you to do is gain from the center of the high and low. You're looking for the rib eye not the whole rib. The low and high on the above example may be $1.07-$1.98 and you just capture the center cut. The idea is nothing goes up in a strait line and you can profit handsomely on this knowledge.

One other point is, as you get a feel for this rotation formula you may want to let the stock float higher (if you have more time to watch it). I feel that silver will sky rocket in the times ahead, making the above example even more exciting.

So that's my strategy for being a weekly trader. Now let's look at one for buy and hold. I am a big fan of small metal exploration companies. Some would call them "penny stocks", but I feel that is a bit demeaning as they are companies that are just small and in some way struggling to get the metal out of the ground. I think these types of stocks are the best bet for any investor. Here are a couple of reasons why.

The upside potential is much greater in these exploration stocks. What you find with many of them is that they may already be getting some silver and other metals out of the ground, but just on a much smaller scale. Also many of them will own a lot of land with staked claims in various parts of the world that are being drilled and are awaiting results. The upside potential then becomes two fold in these stocks. First, they benefit from a rise in the underlying metal such as silver just as the big mining operations, and from the much anticipated drill results. Both of which can move the stock price. And yet one more dimension to add is the possibility of a minor company such as these becoming takeover targets. Large mining companies are always on the lookout for new mining interests and may make a bid for one of these little guys which can jump the share price a lot. In fact, I think it could be said that large mining companies are forced into acquiring new finds as their long standing mines are being depleted. And the final dimension as I see it is the low cost of these stocks, say from 20 cents to $1.50 a share.

At this point we need to talk about risk. As with any small company in any field there will be risk. A company can go bankrupt for a number of reasons. A few that would be unique to the mining sector would be poor drill results or lack of financing to build the mine. Both of which could cause a drop in share price.

So let's say you have 10,000.00 dollars to invest and you decide to put it into my favorite blue chip silver stock SSRI.

- ✓ SSRI is currently trading at 32 dollars a share. You could buy around 312 shares and let's say silver has a big jump and SSRI goes up five dollars a share you would make roughly fifteen hundred dollars.

Not bad, but lets look at what might have happened had you placed that same 10,000.00 into say 3 exploration companies.

- ✓ Stock A is .74 and you purchase 4504 shares
- ✓ Stock B is .23 and you purchase 14,491 shares
- ✓ Stock C is .39 and you purchase 8546 shares

All three would benefit from the rise in silver but let's say that a short time after the silver rise stock A and C announce fabulous drill results proving up a lot of silver per ton of ore, and stock B becomes a takeover target of SSRI.

- ✓ Stock A increases to $ 1.37
- ✓ Stock B increases to .98
- ✓ Stock C increases to $1.11

It does not seem all that impressive as compared to the five dollar gain in SSRI as we saw above. But let's look at it.

- ✓ Stock A we had 4504 shares from our $3333.00 investment it is now worth $6170.00 for a profit of $2837.00.
- ✓ Stock B we had 14,491 shares it is now worth $14,201.00 for a profit of 10.868.00.
- ✓ Stock C we had 8546 shares it is now worth $9486.00 for a profit of $6153.00.

You started with ten thousand, you made a total profit of $19,858.00+ 10,000, your original investment puts $29,858.00 back into your account. You may reinvest it into other exploration companies or simply wait to see if the price of stock A, B, or C comes back down and jump in again.

Here is a formula you should memorize

> 1 cent move on 100 shares is 1 dollar
> 1 cent move on 1000 shares is 10 dollars
> 1 cent move on 10,000 shares is 100 dollars
> 1 cent move on 100,000 shares is 1000 dollars

Obviously this would work best on lower priced stocks as it would be difficult to purchase 100,000 shares of a 10 dollar stock. This would cost 1 million dollars. If you were to buy 100,000 shares of a 9 cent stock it would only cost 9000 dollars or if you just bought 10,000 shares it would only cost 900 dollars. Not bad considering your upside potential.

The key is how much time you are willing to spend and what you are willing to sacrifice. Are you willing to give up watching TV to spend time studying these markets? I have found it to be both enjoyable and rewarding. It is truly fun when your hard work yields profits.

Investing does not have to be a nerve racking experience. When you invest in tangibles, as I believe metal stocks are, you can sleep well at night knowing you have invested wisely and not on pure euphoria as many of the dot coms were. By being a weekly trader you are one who is diligent about your investments and not afraid to make a trade when you have a profit, nor are you worried when it goes down some. You have a long term focus and realize that metals are the investment of the present and the future. Trading using the patterns discussed above may be the best way to profit from what I believe the future holds.

CHAPTER 11

My Top Ten and Why

The first stocks I want to talk about are the one's that have the word silver in the company's name. It is my belief that as the euphoria for silver takes off the investing community will first jump on stocks that clearly indicate what they do. It may seem silly to a seasoned investor, but you know as well as I that Wall Street is anything but rational and when the feeding frenzy kicks in, look out.

Stocks with "silver" in name
AGQ.V Arian Silver
ASGMF.OB Avino Silver and Gold
ECU.V ECU Silver Mining
ECU.V ECU Silver Mining
EDR.TO Endeavour Silver
EPZ.V Esperanza Silver
FR.V First Majestic Silver
FVI.V Fortuna Silver Mines
HDA.V Huldra Silver
IPT.V Impact Silver
KS.V Klondike Silver
MAG.V MAG Silver
MSV.TO Minco Silver
OK.V Orko Silver
PJO.V Palmarejo Silver and Gold
SBB.V Sabina Silver
SDRG.OB Silver Dragon

Stocks with "silver" in name
SLW Silver Wheaton
SSRI Silver Standard Resources
SVG.V Silver Grail
SVL.V Silvercrest Mines
SVM.TO Silvercorp Metals

Below is a long list of companies whose main focus may not be silver but often have substantial silver resources. This is a diverse list of metals including zinc, copper, uranium, molybdenum, lead and every other metal you can think of including gold.

Other Metal Stocks of Great Interest
ABI.V Abcourt Mines (Silver, Zinc)
ADA.V Acadian Gold (Gold, Zinc)
AEM Anico Eagle Mines (Silver)
AGXM Argentex Mining (Silver, Gold, Indium, Zinc, Copper, Lead)
ARU.V Aurelian Resources (Gold, Copper)
AUA.V Adenac Moly Corp (Molybdenum)
AUN.V Aurcana Corp (Silver, Zinc, Copper)
AUY Yamana Gold (Gold)
AVL.V Avalon Ventures (Beryllium, Lithium, Feldspars, Tantalum)
AZK Aurizon Mines (Gold, Uranium)
BAY.V Bayswater Uranium (Uranium)
BCM.V Bear Creek Mining Gold, Silver)
CCJ Cameco CP (Uranium)
CDE Coeur D Alene (Silver, Gold)
CFTN.PK Clifton Mining (Silver)
CHX.V Cash Minerals (Uranium)
CML.V Crowflight Minerals (Nickel)
CRD.V Caronado Resources (Copper, silver)
CRMXF.OB Cream Minerals (Diamonds)
CS.TO Capstone Mining (Copper, Silver, Zinc)
CUP Peru Copper (Copper, Gold, Silver, Molybdenum)
CZN.TO Canadian Zinc (Zinc Silver)

Other Metal Stocks of Great Interest
DEN.TO Denison Mines (Uranium)
DLKM.OB Douglas Lake Minerals (Gold)
EFR.V Energy Fuels (Uranium, Vanadium)
EMC.TO Energy Metals (Uranium)
EPM.TO European Minerals (Gold, Copper)
EXN.V Excellon Resources (Silver)
FAN.TO Farallon Resources (Zinc)
FNI.V First Nickel (Nickel)
FNX.TO FNX Mining (Nickel, Copper, Platinum, Palladium, Gold)
FR.V First Majestic (Silver)
FRG Fronteer Development
FSY.TO Forsys Metals (Uranium, Gold, Copper, Zinc)
FV.V Firestone Ventures (Zinc, Gold, Uranium)
GGC.V Genco Resources (Silver, Gold)
GGC.V Genco Resources (Silver, Gold)
GMO Idaho General Mines   (Molybdenum)
GORO.OB Gold Resource Corp (Gold, Silver)
GPR.V Great Panther Resources (Silver)
GPXM.OB Golden Phoenix Minerals (Molybdenum)
GRG.V Golden Arrow Resources (Gold)
GRS Gammon Lake Resources (Gold)
HBM.TO HudBay Minerals (Zinc, Copper)
HER.AX Herald Resources
IAU.TO Intrepid Mines (Gold, Silver)
IMR IMA Exploration (Silver, Lead)
INV.TO International Nickel Ventures (Nickel)
KBR.TO Kimber Resources (Gold)
KMK.V Continental Mineral (Gold, Copper)
KRE.V Kenrich- Eskay Mining (Gold, Silver, Copper, Lead, Zinc)
LBE.V Liberty Mines (Nickel)
LMC Lundin Mining (Zinc, Copper)
LRG.V Lateegra Gold (Gold, Silver)
LSG.TO Lake Shore Gold (Gold)

Other Metal Stocks of Great Interest
MAI.V Minera Andes Corp (Gold, Silver)
MFM.V Marifil Mines (Gold, Silver)
MFN Minefinders Ltd (Silver gold)
MGN Mines Management (Silver, Copper)
MMG Metaline Mining   (Zinc and silver)
MNV.V Mexivada Mining (Gold, Silver, Diamond, Uranium, Molybdenum)
MTO.V Metanor Resources (Gold)
MUN.TO Mundoro Mining (Gold) China
MXR.V Max Resources
NAK Northern Dynasty Minerals (Copper, Gold, Molybdenum)
NI.TO Victory Nickel (Nickel)
NME.V Namex Exploration (Silver, Gold, Zinc, Nickel, Platinum, Cobalt,
NOT.V Noront Resources ((Gold)
NPG.V Nevada Pacific Gold (Silver, Gold)
NSM.V Northern Star Mining (Gold)
NUX.V New Pacific Metals (Silver, Gold Copper, Nickel, Cobalt, Platinum)
NWT.V Northwestern Mineral Ventures (Uranium, Silver, Gold)
ORM.V Oremex Resources (Gold, Silver, Lead, Zinc)
OTMN.PK O.T. Mining (Gold)
PAX.V Pacifica Resources (Zinc, Lead)
PDN.TO Paladin Resources (Uranium)
PLE.V Plexmar Resources (Silver, Gold)
RMKMF.PK Roxmark Mines (Gold, Molybdenum)
RNO Rio Narcea Gold Mine (Gold, Nickel, Silver)
RVM.TO Revett Minerals (Silver, Copper)
SAM.V Starcore (Gold, Silver)
SKV.V Skygold Ventures (Gold)
SMM.AX Summit Resources (Uranium, Vanadium, Copper, Gold)
SPM.TO Scorpio Mining (Silver, Gold, Zinc, Lead, Copper)
SRLM.PK Sterling Mining (Silver)
SST.V Silverstone Resources (Silver, Gold)
STM.V Strathmore Minerals (Uranium)
SXR.TO SXR Uranium One (Uranium, Gold)

Other Metal Stocks of Great Interest
TUMIF.OB Tumi Resources (Silver, Gold)
URA.V Anglo Canadian Uranium (Uranium, Gold, Copper, Palladium)
URRE.OB Uranium Resources (Uranium)
URZ Uranerz Energy (Uranium)
USA.V Chrysalis Capital III (Silver, Lead
UUL.V Universal Uranium (Uranium)
UUU.V Urasia Energy (Uranium)
WGI.TO Western Goldfields (Gold)

One reason why I really like metal stocks below 40 cents (US) is that when they go up your percentage gains can be fantastic. One thing to look at is why is the price so low? Are they just a tiny exploration company with potential or has something, that might soon change, beaten the stock price down. Another thing I look at is if the company seems solid. Your downside risk may be less because it just can't go any lower without going bankrupt. Bankruptcy is always a risk, but again if it looks solid and has a good track record it may well be worth taking a chance. Every company has to start somewhere.

Metal Stocks below 40 cents (US)
AIM.AX AIM Resources (Zinc, Copper, Gold)
AMS.V Amera Resources (Gold, Silver, Copper)
CCE.V Commerce Resources (Tantalum, Niobium)
CQ.V Cooper Minerals (Uranium)
DKGR.PK Drake Gold Resources (Gold, Silver)
HEG.AX Hill End Gold (Gold)
KNP.V Knight Resources (Nickel)
MAR.AX Malachite Resources (Gold, Silver, Copper)
MGA.V Mega Uranium (Uranium)
NAG.V North American Gem (Uranium, Molybdenum, Gold, Copper)
NMB.V Normabec Mining (Silver, Gold)
RPT.V Rampart Ventures (Uranium)
SDRC.PK Sidney Resources (Silver, Gold)
SLGLF.OB Silverado Gold Mines (Gold) (Enviro. friendly fuel from coal)
SLT.V Solitaire Minerals (Gold, Copper, Molybdenum, Uranium)
SNR.V Senator Minerals (Gold, Silver, Molybdenum, Copper)
THR.AX Thor Mining (Tungsten, Molybdenum, Uranium)

There are many more mining companies out there that I have not mentioned in this book. Some perhaps I just am not aware of others are just too expensive already. One strong criterion I use is I will not even mention a company that hedges. A company that hedges sells forward its metals before they have mined them, often for a deep loss compared to what they could have realized for them. There are several reasons a company will do this but I am of the opinion that this practice is unethical, immoral and downright shortsighted showing little faith in the product they produce. An end result of this is that a stock will remain flat or even go down in a bull market because the market realizes they have hedged and are not benefiting from the rise in the underlying metal. So if you don't see a particular company in the ones listed above, do some research to find out if they have hedged. To the best of my knowledge all companies mentioned in this book are hedge free.

There are several good gold mining companies out there, but many have hedged and are floundering because of it. In many cases gold mines also have substantial silver resources. The same thing that I said about silver can also be true for gold, if it has gold in its name it may be picked first. Below are a few of my favorites.

Gold Mining Companies
GG Goldcorp
NXG Northgate Minerals
TRGD.PK Tara Gold

Top Ten List

OK, that gives you a lot to pick from but it must be said that this is by no means a complete list of all mining companies. So now let's narrow it down to my top 10. The list below was very difficult to narrow down. What I tried to do since this book will become dated very quickly as financial markets move fast, was to put together a list of companies that I feel are solid, affordable and have a lot of future potential. That is not to say that many of the other stocks mentioned in this chapter don't meet this same criteria. This list of ten stocks I feel you could potentially buy them and forget about them for years and they would not only still be around but would be worth substantially more than you paid for them.

SSRI Silver Standard Resources.[53]

This company in my opinion is the "silver standard". They meet most of the criteria I feel is important for me to invest in a silver company. They are not hedged. They have silver in their name. They have projects all over the world which limits their exposure to just one country and they are a current producer as well as having many exploration projects. Perhaps the biggest downfall to this company at this time would be that because it is so large and well known to silver investors its stock price is currently around 30 dollars a share. This makes it difficult to buy very many shares. Just to purchase 100 shares would cost you 3000 dollars making it difficult for most to make a good profit on a percentage basis.

MFN Minefinders Corp.[54]

This one has been a favorite of mine for a long time. This is a company with a lot of proven reserves that has been in business for over thirty years giving it a long proven track record. Its mines are located in the safe areas of North America. It is a current producer of silver, gold and other metals as well as having many exploration projects. The company is well known for having joint ownership with other companies which can be very beneficial as it can limit exposure if drill results are poor as well as giving the opportunity to buy out the interests of the joint partner if the project turns out to be a good one. It is unhedged and has a current stock price in the 9 dollar range making it a little easier to realize good profits for less investment capital than SSRI.

SDRG.OB Silver Dragon[55]

This one just recently became a favorite. It has silver in its name and a catchy name but these would not be the main reasons. A basic profile on the company is that it currently has 11 different projects going from Mexico to China. It just recently poured its first silver bar in China at the Erbahuo Silver Mine. This company gives you exposure to the Chinese market, which at this point is far from common in silver mining.

SVG.V Silver Grail[56]

This is a small exploration company with a lot of potential. It is a top recommendation of Jason Hommel of the Silver Stock Report, one of the newsletters I subscribe to, as well as being a substantial holding of his multi-million dollar portfolio. The company has nine silver projects going. I consider it cheap with this many projects for .70 US a share. Often you see exploration companies with just one or two projects in the same price range.

The company owns a lot of land and I believe the future is very bright for this company. This is one stock, because of its low price you could make a very good percentage gain.

SRLM.OB Sterling Mining [57]

This company has been around since 1903. It has several properties in the US and Mexico, most famous of which is the Sunshine Mine in Idaho. It is primarily a silver company. It has properties within two legendary silver districts the Zacatecas silver district in Mexico where it owns over 18,000 acres and the silver valley extending from Idaho to Montana and has nearly 20,000 acres in this region. Current stock price in the 3 dollar range.

CFTN.PK Clifton Mining [58]

This company is located in perhaps one of the safest mining areas in the world located on the border between Utah and Nevada, it owns 5,100 acres in this rich mining district. It also owns a portion of American Biotech labs the producer of ASAP the silver nano product I mention in the silver health chapter. This company has a lot of potential and is another one with a stock price currently below a dollar a share.

CZN.TO Canadian Zinc [59]

I like this company for two reasons; first it has a lot of silver reserves and is currently producing silver, second it has a lot of zinc. Most investors could care less about zinc but it is essential in the galvanization of steel as well as other applications. The most compelling argument for this stock is the fact that zinc is in very short supply as its recent price run up indicates. The LME stock warehouse is at an all time low. Its share price as of this writing is bellow a dollar US making it a very good prospect. Its main project is located in the Northwest Territory of Canada.

SVL.V Silvercrest Mines[60]

This company advertises itself as a pure silver play. It has 100% interest in three silver properties in Mexico, El Salvador and Chile. It is an exploration company with a lot of potential. With a current price around 1 dollar a share.

FR.V First Majestic Silver[61]

This company has three active silver mines in Mexico which the company projects will produce 5 million ounces of silver in 2007. It also owns two exploration properties in Mexico. The company has the advantage of already being a producer which speaks to its current stock price in the 5 dollar range.

EDR.TO Endeavour Silver[62]

This company is also a current producer with a projected production of 3.5 million ounces of silver in 2007. It has 2 major projects. The Guanacevi Mines with a history dating back to 1535 by the Spaniards. This district is said to be one of the richest areas of silver in all of Mexico. Its other project, the Parral Mines Project, is in another well known district first discovered in 1631. The company has ongoing aggressive exploration of the Veta Colorada vein system. Current stock price is in the 4 dollar range.

As I have mentioned before, one thing I look for when considering the purchase of a stock is the current price as compared to its 52 week high. If it is at or near its high it may not be the best time to buy it. But of course that is relative to what the underlining metal is doing. If silver is rising fast then these stocks will also and you may just have to jump in if you feel silver is going higher. That having been said, a much better entry point would be one that is closer to its 52 week low—if you can find one.

One final point to remember is that inflation can greatly effect a stocks price. So just because the Dow seems to be doing well, or any individual stock for that matter, you must remember it is a numbers game. The loss in value in the dollar alone can make a stock go up and may have nothing to do with how well a company is doing. This is yet one more reason why I like silver stocks. They will of course benefit from the numbers game, but the true side of this coin is they have intrinsic value and are thus a true store of wealth.

Disclaimer—all of the companies mentioned in this chapter are not outright recommendations, they are merely stocks that I know of and have a lot of potential. Some are very small exploration companies while some are major producers and the rest fall somewhere in-between. I do own or have owned some of these companies, but I trade in and out of stocks all the time and a recommendation would become quickly dated after the publication of this book. Therefore, if you are serious, first do your own research. Nearly all of the companies mentioned in this chapter have websites making research easy. I would recommend subscribing to a good newsletter for more timely recommendations. I have a few of my favorites in the Web sites chapter.

CHAPTER 12

Case Studies

In this chapter we will take an in depth look at some specific stocks and their charts to see what recent price moves can tell us about how the company might perform in the future and how we can profit from it. Before we begin I need to tell what I feel is the most important rule to understand in order to be a good investor, here it is.

Have a deep understanding of percentages.

We will see in the examples that follow why this is so important.

Silver Dragon Resources
Silver Dragon Resources is a favorite of mine. One reason is that it has silver in the company name and second it has good up and down moves and is small enough not to tie up to much capital.

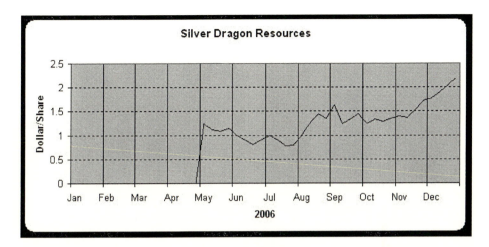

Symbol SDRG.OB

52 Week Range 0.75-2.19   **Average Volume 299,662**

If you had purchased this stock in the summer of 2006 near its low of $0.75 and still held it into December at $2.19 you would have realized a profit of $1.44 a share or 192%.

Silver Standard Resources

Now let's take a look at Silver Standard Resources, perhaps the largest unhedged silver miner out there. If you had bought this one at its year low of $14.93 a share and held it into December as well when it reached $30.42 you would have gained $15.49 per share. This makes the above example look very small, but when we look at it on a percentage basis Silver Standard only returned 103%. It looks a lot bigger, but the fact is the higher the share price at point of entry the harder it is to make a large percentage gain. Also a larger portion of money will have to be tied up for a year to make this 103% as compared with the amount in Silver Dragon for six months to make 192%.

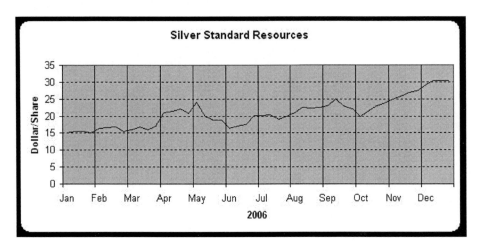

Symbol SSRI

52 Week Range 14.93-30.42   **Average Volume 807,138**

Silver Grail

Silver Grail is another favorite of mine. It has silver in its name and is small enough to make good percentage gains on your money. If you had got into this stock in January at $0.11 and held it into December at $0.92 you would have realized a gain of 736%.

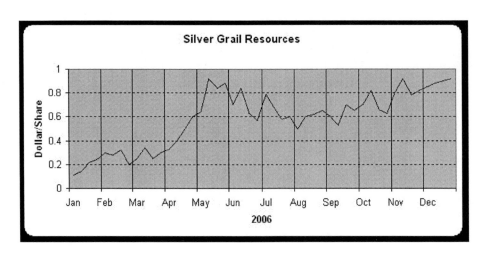

Symbol SVG.V

52 Week Range 0.11-0.92   **Average Volume 49,671**

Silvercrest Mines

Silvercrest Mines has had some nice ups and downs in the past couple of years. You could have purchased it near its low of 61 cents in January 2006 and sold it four months later at its high of $1.85 for a nice gain of $1.24 a share or 203%. This again dipped back down to 65 cents in October and by early December was back up in the $1.25 range for another nice gain of 92%. By looking at the chart you can see it also had several little moves you could have capitalized on.

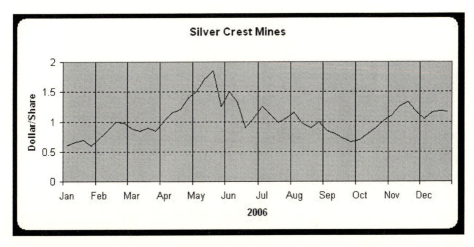

Symbol SVL.V

52 Week Range 0.61-1.85   **Average Volume 60,504**

I want you to get used to reading charts. A great deal of knowledge can be gained. Things like seasonal moves and how one stock does compared to another at a particular period of time can tell you a lot about what it will do in the future.

Clifton Mining

Clifton Mining is a company that has a lot going for it, however as you can see from the chart it has been in a downtrend for the year. If you had bought it at its high for the year of $1.30 you wouldn't be very happy at the end of the year with it in the 60 cent range. Here is where I would like to make the point that *when you buy a stock it is never a loss until you sell it.* If you still believe in the basic fundamentals of the company then just stick with it. It may soon have its day in the sun. It is worth noting that by reading the chart we can see that around August Clifton went into a nice rolling pattern with several 20 to 25 cent moves. This is where you need to keep percentages in mind. A 20 cent move on this one with a buy around 50 cents and sell around 70 cents could give you several nice 40% profits.

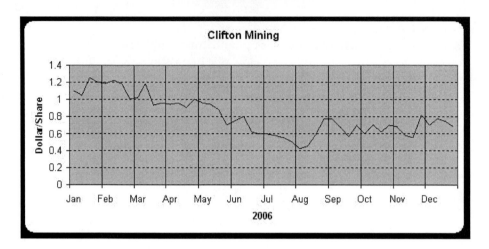

Symbol CFTN.PK

52 Week Range 0.42-1.30   **Average Volume 50,344**

Argentex Mining
Argentex Mining is an interesting company which has recently had a large find of Indium a very rare metal.[63] Had you purchased this stock near its low of 35 cents and still had it at the end of the year at $1.73 you would have had a profit of $1.41 a share or 402%.

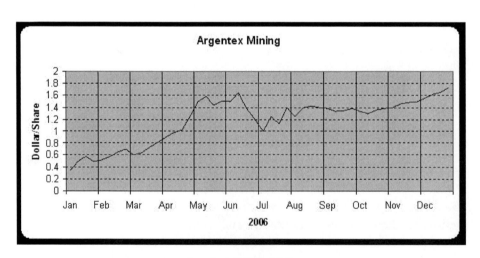

Symbol AGXM.OB

52 Week Range 0.35-1.73   **Average Volume 172,683**

Firestone Ventures
Firestone Ventures is a favorite of mine. This company has a lot of Uranium and Zinc[64] and with a low stock price it has a lot of upside potential. Had you bought this one at its low of 13 cents you could have sold it a few months later at 85 cents for a profit of 72 cents a share or 553%.

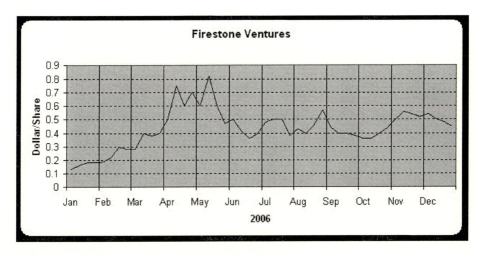

Symbol FV.V

52 Week Range 0.13-0.85   **Average Volume 156,609**

Minefinders Corp.
I have traded in and out of Minefinders Corp more times than I can count. Just take a look at that chart. Talk about ups and downs. This one offers lots of opportunities to make many percentage gains.

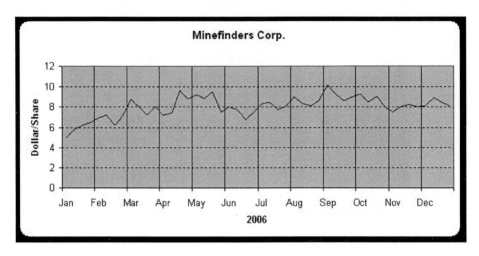

Symbol MFN

52 Week Range 5.00-10.19   **Average Volume 234,900**

Aurcana Corp.

WOW, I would sure like to say I was in Aurcana Corp. at the start of the year! It illustrates with a capital "I" what a mining stock can do when a fire is lit under it. If you had bought it at its low of 5 cents a share and sold at the high of $1.47 you would have realized a profit of an incredible $1.42 a share or 2840%. Let's do some math on this one. If you had placed 5000 dollars into this at 5 cents a share you could have bought 100,000 shares. If you could have resisted the temptation to sell it along the way your 5000 dollar investment would be worth $147,000.00 dollars. These are the kind of returns that can and will in the future be realized by patient investors.

So let's talk about when to sell and when to hold. This is every investor's dilemma. Often I have sold to soon only to watch a stock shoot higher while at other times I thought of taking a profit, didn't and then it falls. The bottom line is you can never go wrong taking a profit, yes it may go higher, but either way you have locked in a profit and there is a lot to be said for that. One rule of thumb to use is if you really think its going higher soon only sell a portion of your holdings, maybe one third, commonly called taking a little off the table. Or you may be able to sell enough to get all your original investment back then you're investing with the profits only. One final point that needs to be made here is that when a mining company makes some big announcement such as drill results there is often a lot of marketplace euphoria that goes along with it. Many people buy into it, often near the top. It has been my experience that when a stock shoots up very fast this is the best time to take a profit and wait on the sidelines for it to come back to earth.

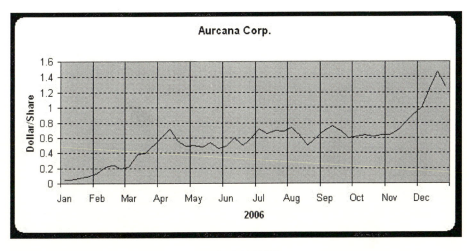

Symbol AUN.V

52 Week Range 0.05-1.47   **Average Volume 528,338**

Silverado Gold Mines
Silverado is another stock with some wild rides. It has a low for the year of
5 cents but has a high of only 60 cents for the year, still a very nice gain of
.55 cents a share or 1100%. As you can see from the chart, it fell back down
at mid year to 5 cents again. I really like this stock. It has a lot going for it.
The average trading volume is 2.3 million shares, which is very high for a
penny stock. It is one of the most traded and most liquid penny stocks. This
company has quite a story. They are primarily a gold mining company; mining
for gold in Alaska. Most of the gold they mine is in the nugget form. One of
the nuggets recovered weighed in at 41.35 ounces of pure gold. Because of
the uniqueness of nugget gold it can be sold to jewelers at a 33% premium
over spot bullion price.[65]

Perhaps even more exciting than this is what they call green fuel. Silverado
Green Fuel Inc. is a wholly owned subsidiary. It possesses a formula for
converting low-rank coal into liquid fuel which is environmentally friendly. It
can be produced for less than 15 dollars a barrel and can be easily converted
into gasoline, diesel, jet fuel, synthetic natural gas and a lot more.[66] Notice in
the chart bellow that this stock has a lot of daily volume. You will also notice
that the volume spikes along with the share price. This can be a predictor
of the upcoming direction of the price as you see the volume getting larger
and larger with each trading day. It also means the stock is very liquid and
it is very easy to get in and out. This can sometimes be a problem on low
volume stocks so it should be considered before a purchase. Often a low

volume stock, say one bellow 25,000 shares traded daily may be more difficult to sell. It is usually not a problem to get your order filled the difficulty will be on the sell side, so when purchasing a low volume stock consider the fact that this may be one you will have to hold a little while. This is not the case with Silverado. It has ample volume and with a stock price below 10 cents, I don't think you can go wrong on this one.

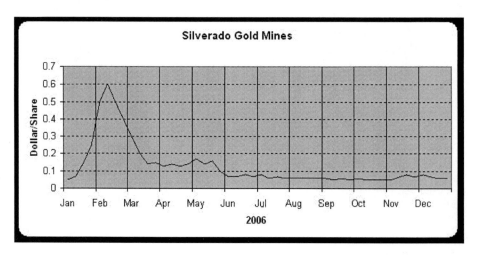

Symbol SLGLF.OB

52 Week Range 0.05-0.60   **Average Volume 4,983,530**

Senator Minerals Inc.
Senator Minerals is another low priced stock I like a lot. As I talked about before in these low priced companies you can make good profits on just a one cent move. You are able to buy a lot more shares than in a 5 or 10 dollar stock. With swings between 10 and 50 cents the potential is there. Senator is a junior exploration company with emphasis on North America. Their most promising prospect is Ivanhoe Creek gold silver target.[67]

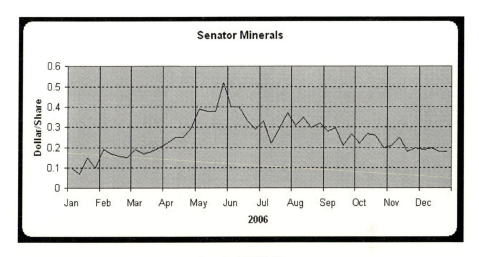

Symbol SNR.V

52 Week Range 0.10-0.52   **Average Volume 90,245**

Liberty Mineral

One word—Nickel. Liberty is the most exciting nickel find to come along in years. It is a recent producer of nickel from its Redstone mine in Ontario Canada. It has several other properties with 12,000 acres of land claims. Nickel supply is at an all time low and this company stands to profit a great deal from this fact.[68]

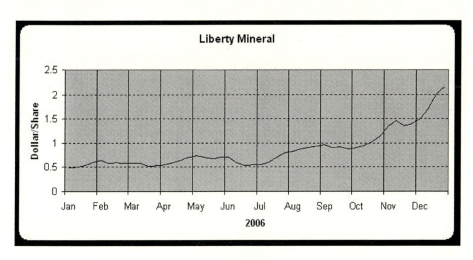

Symbol LBE.V

52 Week Range 0.49-2.17   **Average Volume 392,781**

Bayswater Uranium

Uranium is one metal that is a must if we are to continue to grow the world's population. It is the essential ingredient in a nuclear reactor. I feel nuclear power is necessary to keep up with the world's power demands. We may not like it but the fact remains. Bayswater has land holdings in Canada's two most important mining and exploration regions the Athabasca Basin and the Thelon Basin.[69] This company has a great future and if Uranium interests you this would be one stock to consider.

This stock has had a couple of nice rotations. You could have bought in mid August at $1.10 and sold about 3 weeks latter at $1.60 for a profit of 50 cents a share or 45%. It slid bellow a dollar in mid October where you could have picked it up again at 80 cents held it for two weeks and sold at $1.40 for a profit of 60 cents a share or 75%. It's never a bad idea to take a profit when one is there. Yes, it could go higher, but there are other stocks out there that may be at a low while this one is at a high.

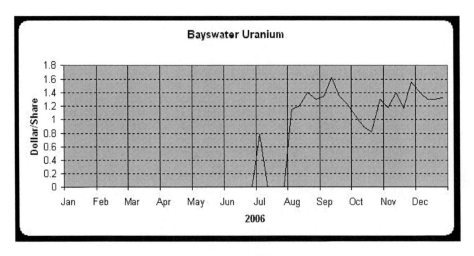

Symbol BAY.V
52 Week Range 0.78-1.69   **Average Volume 762,889**

Canadian Zinc Corp.

Canadian Zinc is a stock that has had some very nice rotations. You could have bought and sold this company several times for some nice profits. Most investors could care less about zinc. It is not a metal one thinks about when investing, but zinc is in very short supply and as the cost of this base metal has increased over the last couple of years it has not brought on any significant new supply.[70] This can be said of many metals, including silver, the price was low for so long very few new projects were started as no profit could be made. As the price of metals has increased, exploration has begun on many projects. It takes 5 to 10 years to bring a discovery to production and because of this zinc will remain in short supply for years to come.

This company also has a lot of silver. Now this is a story. Canadian Zinc purchased the Prairie Creek Mine in 1994 located in the Northwestern Territories of Canada.[71] For any history buffs out there, this mine is the infamous one that the Hunt brothers, William and Bunker, owned in 1980 when they attempted to corner the silver market and drove the price of silver to fifty dollars an ounce.[72]

According to the company prospectus they have 51,370,000 recoverable ounces of silver and 3 billion dollars worth of mine able zinc.[73] That is a lot for your money, considering a stock price bellow a dollar a share.

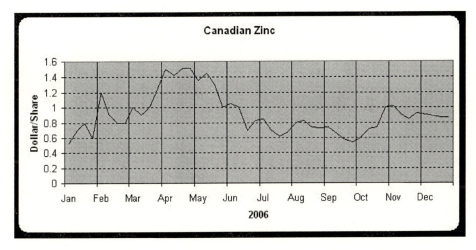

Symbol CZN.TO

52 Week Range 0.53-1.63   **Average Volume 380,477**

There are many theories out there on how to predict the future move in a stock by studying a chart, most of which I find totally ineffective for mining stocks. So much is dependant on the price of the underlying metal and how much of it they have or may yet find. I look at a chart to see where a stock has been as somewhat of a predictor as where it might go. I do not place much weight on this predictor. *The real predictors will be revealed in your own research*. When using charts the following items are useful to help you make your buy and sell decisions.

Percentage moves—Keeping your focus on a stock percentage move is important. It may look like you made more money on a higher priced stock while in reality you could have made a lot more simply due to the fact that you are able to purchase more shares of a lower priced stock. Capitalizing on percentage moves enables you to make more money in the long run.

Volume—This can tell you a lot about how much interest there is in the stock. How many shares change hands each day. This can also tell you how much a stock has moved upward on a volume spike, often after some news has come out on the company.

52 week range—All of the charts above are 52 week charts or 1 year charts. Charts are also available with longer periods such as 2 to 5 years. The 52 week format is the time period I use most to see rotation patterns to help me make buying decisions. The chart can also help you to find an undervalued stock or one that is in a dip and is closer to its 52 week low than its 52 week high. As I've stated before try not to buy at the top. Take the time to determine where the company has been in the last year. I also find it helpful to look at a one month chart. It will give you a lot more detail than we saw in the charts above. If you become a weekly trader the one month chart will show you the most recent moves of the stock and can help guide you in your buying and selling decisions.

I am not a big fan of charting services that charge you to have access to their charts and predictions. There are many charts available for free. They give you the basic information you need without the things that don't really help you much with metal stocks. Utilizing the predictors revealed in your research and the charting techniques mentioned will aid you in your buying and selling decisions.

alloy that combines zinc and copper is perhaps the best known alloy. Prestal an alloy containing 78% zinc and 22% aluminum is a strategic material that is nearly as strong as steel but is molded as easily as plastic. Zinc Oxide is used in paints, rubber products, cosmetics, pharmaceuticals, plastics, printing inks, soap and batteries.[81]

Cobalt
Cobalt is used in many industrial applications such as leveling devices and thickness gauges as well as radiotherapy in hospitals. It is increasingly being used for sterilization of spices and certain foods. The powerful gamma rays kill bacteria and other pathogens, without damaging the product. After the radiation ceases the product is not left radioactive. This is a process sometimes called "cold pasteurization".[82]

Indium
Indium is an interesting industrial metal. It has a low melting point of 313.8 degrees farenheight making it ideal for many applications including as a coating for high speed ball bearings, solar cells, mirrors, regulators in nuclear power and photo cells.[83]

Beryllium
Beryllium is a metal with many uses, especially in Aerospace. It is lighter than Aluminum but stiffer than steel. It is a good electrical and thermal conductor and is non-magnetic.[84]

Lithium
Lithium is the lightest known metal, it has many applications including batteries, aircraft, spacecraft and as a medication to treat manic depression disorder.[85]

Feldspars
Feldspar is by far the most abundant group of minerals in the earths crust. It is primarily used in industrial applications for its alumina and alkali content. Most of the products we use on a daily basis are made with feldspar including glass, fiberglass for insulation, floor tiles and tableware just to name a few of its uses.[86]

Tantalum
Tantalum is a strong, ductile metal that is nearly immune to chemical attack at room temperatures. It can be drawn into a fine wire that is used to evaporate metals such as aluminum. It has a high melting point and is frequently used as a substitute for platinum which is more expensive. It is used to make

components for chemical plants, nuclear power plants, airplanes and missiles. Tantalum does not react with body fluids and thus is used to make surgical equipment, sutures, implants such as artificial joints and cranial plates.[87]

Vanadium
Vanadium is a corrosion resistant metal often used to make tubes and pipes for the chemical industry. It does not easily absorb neutrons and has some applications in the nuclear power industry.[88]

Niobium
Niobium is used as an alloying agent, and for jewelry. Its most interesting application is its use in the field of superconductivity. It is blended with zirconium to make superconductive magnets.[89]

Tungsten
Tungsten is a very hard, heavy metal and has the highest melting point of all non-alloyed metals. This fact makes it the ideal metal for use in light bulb filaments and x-ray tubes. Its high melting point makes it an ideal metal for the demands of a spacecraft.[90]

Palladium
Palladium is a soft silver white metal which has a low melting point. The largest use of this metal today is in catalytic converters. As with gold palladium can be beaten into very thin leaf form as thin as 100 nm.[91]

Platinum
Platinum has unique chemical and physical properties that make it essential in a wide on industrial and environmental applications. And yet it is considered one of the finest jewelry metals. Platinum is the "Most Precious, precious metal. It is the rarest of all precious metals. In contrast with gold and silver, there are no large above ground platinum stockpiles to protect against significant supply disruptions. Approximately 10 tons of raw ore must be mined to produce just one ounce of metal.[92]

Base metals are a form of money; hence the reason smaller denomination coins were made out of copper and nickel. While these metals are not rare it still takes effort to extract them from the ground, which gives them tangible value. I believe the general populace is beginning to awaken to the fact that money should be made of, or at least backed by something tangible. The best way to profit from this is diversify into some base metal stocks as well as looking for silver miners that have base metals in plenty.

Chapter 14

Raw Survival

Through the prompting of a few friends, I decided to include a chapter on survival. It is my belief that we are headed for some very hard times in this country. I am by nature a pessimist. My wife is the optimist in our relationship, so at times she looks at me a bit funny. For the most part it works out well as she helps to keep me toned down. At times, a very good thing!

When most of us think about survival we think about someone holed up in some cabin in the wilds of Canada, or the burly bearded mountain man who climbs Mount Everest. This is not the type of survival I am talking about. What I am talking about is worse case scenarios—how to prepare for and survive them. Below are a few scenarios of real situations that could happen to an ordinary guy or gal.

- Job loss
- Hyperinflation
- Currency crisis
- Nuclear or biological attack
- Breadwinner leaves or dies
- Natural disaster—hurricane, earthquake, tornado, drought
- Power grid failure

Any one of these could befall us, but the ones I would like to elaborate on are the financial ones—job loss, hyperinflation and currency crisis. We have explored at length the topics of being debt free and having tangible assets on hand, but now lets get down to basic human needs. There may come a time when certain items may be more valuable than silver or gold. Below is a breakdown of items you may want to consider purchasing and storing away.

Protection

o Shotgun or rifle with extra ammo. To me the perfect weapon against home invasion is the shotgun. If there is one sound all criminals know it is the sound of a racking shotgun. I'm not a big fan of handguns, it is much easier for a child to be harmed by a handgun, and, if push came to shove, in the dark you have a much greater chance of downing an assailant with a shotgun than a handgun. The old saying goes, spray and pray.

o A big part of protection is safety. Knowledge is power and ignorance equals weakness. Teach your family how to protect themselves, give them skills. Learn some martial arts skills, take a hunters safety class. If you are going to protect your family with a firearm, you need them to understand the true danger it can be, if it is used incorrectly. WE need to make our children aware that death is final. Our children see over and over actors on TV and in the movies die and then are alive again in another show. In their minds death is temporary. Video games encourage kill or be killed. They shoot over and over again and then start a new game. Death is not reality to them. WE need to instill this knowledge into them with passion and zeal. Their life may depend on it. Take them out in the woods, line up some watermelons and shoot them. Explain to them the damage that can be done to the human body and if that was a persons head, they are not coming back. Our kids need a little shock therapy on this very important issue.

Food

o Food Supply—The average household in America is lucky if it has one week food supply on hand. I would suggest upping that to at least a three month supply and gradually increase it to a two year supply. Start with nonperishables such as can goods, pasta and dry soup mixes. Make sure to buy things you know you will eat.

o Appliances—Consider buying a freezer, if you don't have one, and stock it with meat.

o Fresh foods—Consider taking up gardening, it is amazing how much you can grow in a very small area even on a small city lot. Learn about foods that grow in the wild (berries, greens, mushrooms etc).

Toiletries

o Hygiene necessities—I don't know about you but I can't imagine life without toilet paper. May sound funny but if it is hard to find on store shelves, a small supply in your basement will be a Godsend.

o   Toothpaste, how happy would you be if you couldn't brush your teeth? If you're a guy like me who goes on camping and hunting trips and can rough it a little, you may go a day or two but beyond that would be disgusting.

o   Shampoo, bar soap, I think this should go without saying one day is too long. Deodorant—need I say more?

Water

o   Source of water—If you have a well then you are all set as long as there is power to run it. A vast number of people are on city water with fluoride in it. City water is just plain ugly. They say if you put it under a microscope you can see fragments of toilet paper. In our age of recycling everything, I don't know if recycled water is such a good idea. To think the water that many drink is recycled raw sewage is not a nice thought. Seems to me we are putting a lot of faith in chlorine and waste treatment plants as well as our government, who sets the standards of how many parts per million of a certain toxin is allowable for human consumption.

o   Water purifier—If you can't get away from city water you may want to consider a more advanced water filtration system such as the Berkey Water Filter, which has silver in its final filter stage to kill off any remaining bacteria. Iodine is another option, if things get bad with the water supply. The military has been using it for years to make even swamp water safe for drinking. Just 20 drops will usually do the trick.[93]

o   Establish a plan—You really need a plan to ensure safe drinking water. When the local water treatment plant issues, boil water or do not consume warnings, you need to know what to do with the brown stuff coming out of your tap. This is one thing very few will be immune from, even upscale multi million dollar communities often get their water from the city. I would suggest having at least 14 gallons of water per person on hand. Remember the human body can survive for weeks without food but only days without water.

Fuel/Power

o   A generator is a must—We all remember well the power grid failure of a few years ago. It would be wise to be well prepared for any interruptions whether they occur from a storm or something else.

o   Fuel/ gas or diesel is needed to run the generator and your vehicles. Remember how crazy people went during that very short power outage—long lines at gas stations and people fighting for the last gallon of gas. Fuel pumps don't work when there is no power! Have ample supply on hand. It will last a while with an additive in it and just rotate it in your vehicle every so often and get fresh. May be a bit of trouble but not as much as not being able to get it when you need it most.

o   Batteries of all sizes. Have an ample supply of these on hand to power flashlights, radios and other things.

o   Lighting—Oil burning lamps are cheap. I just bought a nice one for 7 dollars and a gallon of ultra clean burning oil for 13 dollars.

o   Cooking—One of the cheapest and easiest is the old fashion camping stove, almost everyone has one lying around somewhere. Also, several of the small propane tanks to run it. This could be a real lifesaver when you find yourself in a tough spot. How lost would many of us be if we could not use our microwaves.

Heating

o   Alternative heating source—You should consider what you would do if there were disruptions with your heat source. Disruptions can be caused by natural gas pipeline breaks, or disruptions in propane and heating oil supplies. You need a backup plan. Heating with wood could be a good alternative. If you have the cash, they now have wood burning stoves that are contained outdoors and heat through a water system.[94] They can also be utilized to produce electricity. An indoor wood burner may be more economical, or upgrading an existing fireplace with an insert to make it more efficient.

o   If you have the ability to stock up on extra fuel this would be a great place to place some extra cash, you know the price will continue to rise. Keep your propane or heating oil tank full, or consider having another one on hand and fill it as well. Unfortunately there is no way to store natural gas.

Health Care/First Aid

o   Medication—this is a big one. Many people are on medications that they cannot be without such as cardiac and blood pressure meds. It would be very wise indeed, if you fall into this category to have at least a three months supply at all times, even if your insurance won't pay for it. It would be money well spent if any interruption in supply were to occur.

o   Vitamins—This goes along with staying healthy and a good supply put away is a good idea.

o   Large First Aid Kit—It's hard to say what interruptions might occur in the health care system, but one thing I see from my perspective is that Emergency Rooms and EMS will be overwhelmed in a national emergency. You should consider such services as your last resort and have yourself prepared to take care of many situations on your own.

Communication
o   Backup plan—You need to consider the fact that cell phones and land lines could go down and be useless. This is not an easy one to have a backup plan for. Our world depends on communication to function. This more than anything I believe could cause mass chaos. Not knowing what is going on when we are so used to having second by second information and contact with loved ones is a bad scenario.
o   Alternative equipment—Short distance hand held radios and CB radios may be lifesavers, as well as having a radio that operates on batteries as well as a shortwave radio.

Job Skills
o   Plan—It may be a good idea to start working toward some skills that could help you in the future. This goes along with having a backup plan. Not just skills to help you get along but skills that could give you access to another source of income.
o   Potential training—First Aid or EMT; Mechanic; Agricultural; Building trade. This is by no means an exhaustive list but just a place to start. There is a wealth of information out there, if you look for it including government web sites, which makes me want to do it all the more.

I have recently taken a sociology class and I learned that modern sociologists are telling us that the United States, Canada and much of Europe are now postindustrial nations that subsist on economies that are based on technology and service, and that is just fine and all is well. I have a real problem with that. Can we really maintain our current standard of living with no manufacturing base? I just don't see it. Call me nieve or undereducated, but to me this is one area we are not using common sense. If a country no longer makes anything it consumes and supports itself with service jobs which can easily be outsourced or covered by imported workers who will do the job for less, what will sustain the country? Am I missing something? I don't think I am. This is why things are so rocky and why I believe we are headed for what will end in a total elimination of the middle class. When you can buy everything you need at China-Mart dirt cheap, made by someone who makes a quarter an hour, your common sense should kick into high gear and realize this is not good. It just really irks me that we have allowed a communist country to steel our financial freedom.

Yet one more reason why I feel we should be prepared for every contingency is that our government is telling us too. I believe they know a whole lot more than they are letting on. Have you looked at their web site, ready.gov it is unbelievable. Just the other day I passed a large billboard telling us to *get ready be prepared*. They have run radio spots, TV spots, and ads in the front page of our phone book. I have even seen flyers at the post office all saying the same thing "you need to be ready and have these items on hand in case of a national emergency". Conspiracy theories abound on 911 and Okalahoma City, some saying that our government had a hand in them. I don't know about their accuracy, but I do know it is prudent to have a plan and to plan ahead. More than ever we need to put ourselves into survival mode.

CONCLUSION

It has been a truly passionate experience for me to write this book. There are precious few times in ones life that a dream can come true. Completing and having it published is indeed a dream come true. To be able to write on a topic that I feel so passionately about and to get the message out there to all who would take the time to read it is the fulfillment of a lifelong dream.

It is my hope that you will take what I have written to heart and put it into practice. I pray you did not find this read to depressing, as the topics of finance can be, especially if you are in debt. Please forgive me if I seemed judgmental for that was not my intention. It was my goal and continues to be my goal to help people. To those that know me I am an extrovert and thoroughly enjoy being around people. From the very depths of my being I want you to have a better tomorrow. It has to start with you! One person at a time working toward: being debt free; using honest weights and measures; striving to live the way God intended; and slowly day by day becoming financially independent.

It will not be easy, for in many ways it requires a total lifestyle change. I believe it is imperative as the survival of our country depends on it. If you will put even just a small amount of what I have suggested in these pages into practice you will be tremendously farther ahead in the future than the vast majority of the worlds population.

WEB SITES & REFRENCES

INVESTING

www.silverstockreport.com
www.jamesdinescompany.com
www.paulvaneeden.com
www.jsmineset.com
www.gold-eagle.com
www.kitco.com
www.coloradogold.com
www.cliftonmining.com
www.miningpedia.com
www.silverminers.com
www.silverstrategies.com
www.silverbullreport.com
www.coininfo.com find your local coin dealer

PROVIDENT LIVING

www.highmowingseeds.com
www.organicseed.com
www.americanbiotechlabs.com
www.fluoridealert.org
www.apfn.org
www.naturalrearing.com
www.fluoridedebate.com
www.radioliberty.com
www.standardprocess.com
www.enviromentalcommons.org
www.biogenticservices.com
www.greenpeople.org/seeds.htm
www.leopold.iastate.edu

www.survivalblog.com
www.silverinscripture.com
www.truenews.com
www.danielstimeline.com
www.ready.gov
www.themoneymasters.com
www.dailyreckoning.com

REFERENCES

[1] Oklahoma Statues Title 12. Civil Procedure Chapter 12 Section 686 Mortgage Foreclosure—Deficiency Judgments

[2] themoneymasters.com/quotations.htm

[3] themoneymasters.com/quotations.htm

[4] themoneymasters.com/quotations.htm

[5] themoneymasters.com/quotations.htm

[6] themoneymasters.com/quotations.htm

[7] bls.gov US Department of Labor

[8] thirdworldtraveler Unemplotment Rate Deception by Eoghan Stafford Dollars and Sense magazine October 2003

[9] newstarget.com Secret of soil nutrition: Why minerals in soil determine the success or failure of foods Mike Adams

[10] fbts.com/NO-GMO.htm

[11] unix.dfn.org Europe the Debate Over Genetically Modified Organisms

[12] Engineered corn kills monarch butterflies Cornell News May 19 1999

[13] allyou.com What does organic really mean?

[14] Why Do I Ache?/video Dr. R.E. Tent D.C N.D. Ph.D.

[15] holisticmed.com/fluoride/

[16] fluoridealert.org

[17] fluoridedebate.com

[18] jewishvirtuallibrary.org Weights, Measures and Coins

[19] wikipedia.org Talent (weight)

[20] coloradogold.com 1857-200? Don Stott

[21] theatlanticfreepress The Second Great Depression Mike Whitney Feb. 2007

[22] Argentina wikipedia.org Argentina economic crisis (1999-2002)

[23] gata.org Leading Canadian Banker recommends gold, denounces fiat system Jan. 2007

[24] gata.org Leading Canadian Banker recommends gold, denounces fiat system Jan. 2007

[25] gata.org Leading Canadian Banker recommends gold, denounces fiat system Jan. 2007

26 the moneychanger.com
27 The US Constitution on line
28 coloradogold.com Don Stott When? part2
29 silverstockreport.com Jason Homel
30 lingens.com German Inflation 1923
31 pbs.org The German Hyperinflation 1923 Paper Money Adam Smith pp 57-62
32 Silver and Cardero Resource editorial Jason Hommel
33 One douzen silver Investor Mistakes editorial Douglas Kanarowski
34 One douzen silver Investor Mistakes editorial Douglas Kanarowski
35 Future Silver Gold Prices the silverstockreport.com Jason Hommel
36 amsilver.con American Biotech Labs
37 pubmed.gov Persistant silver disinfectant for the environmental control of pathogenic bacteria
38 essaymedical.com/GUIDE.pdf X-static The silver fiber
39 pcgs.com Profesional Coin Grading Service
40 ebay.com/coins
41 usmint.gov The United States Mint
42 usmint.gov The United States Mint
43 coloradogold.com
44 The Red Book Coin Value Guide
45 The Red Book Coin Value Guide
46 The Red Book Coin Value Guide
47 The Red Book Coin Value Guide
48 The Red Book Coin Value Guide
49 usmint.gov The United States Mint
50 cnn.com Auction brings 7.6 million for "Double Eagle
51 worldnetdaily.com Opportunity amidst the tech wreck Bob Howard June 22 2001
52 powells.com Dot.con: How America Lost its Mind and Money in the Internet Era John Cassidy
53 silverstandard.com
54 minefinders.com
55 silverdragonresources.com
56 silvergrail.com
57 sterlingmining.com
58 cliftonmining.com
59 canadianzinc.com
60 silvercrestmines.com
61 firstmajestic.com
62 edrsilver.com
63 argentexmining.com
64 firestoneventures.com

65 silverado.com

66 silverado.com

67 senatorinc.com

68 24hourgold.com Liberty Mines

69 bayswateruranium.com

70 resourceinvestor.com GFMS Analysis Illustrates Bullish case for Zinc John A. Nones Jul. 2006

71 canadianzinc.com

72 goldeagle.com/editorials Japan Asia Investments Special Situation Silver for Free Donald Dross march 2006

73 canadianzinc.com

74 silverstockreport.com Two Moly Stocks Jason Hommel

75 forbes.com Ban the Penny Mark Lewis July 2002

76 chicagofed.org Whats a Penny (or Nickel) Really Worth Francois D.Velede, senior economist

77 The Red Book Coin Value Guide

78 coinflation.com

79 education.jlab.org Its Elemental/Uranium

80 sg.biz.yahoo.com Nickel Hits New High Above 40,000 Anna Stablim Feb. 07

81 education.jlab.org Its Elemental Jefferson Lab/Zinc

82 education.jlab.org Its Elemental Jefferson Lab

83 education.jlab.org Its Elemental Jefferson Lab

84 education.jlab.org Its Elemental Jefferson Lab

85 education.jlab.org Its Elemental Jefferson Lab

86 education.jlab.org Its Elemental Jefferson Lab

87 education.jlab.org Its Elemental Jefferson Lab

88 education.jlab.org Its Elemental Jefferson Lab

89 education.jlab.org Its Elemental Jefferson Lab

90 education.jlab.org Its Elemental Jefferson Lab

91 education.jlab.org Its Elemental Jefferson Lab

92 penoir.com/platinum

93 msucares.com Disaster Preparedness/Water

94 woodsedge.com Heatmaster